THE WAITING ROOM

Wisdom For Waiting Victoriously By Faith!

--------------❖❖❖--------------

Felicia E. Emanuel

Ten-digit ISBN: 0692422781

Thirteen-digit ISBN: 978-0692422786

Published by: FeliciaEmanuel.com

DEDICATION

----❖ ❖ ❖----

This book is dedicated to my two amazing sons: **Eren** *and* **Eric***.*

It is a joy to be your mother and my life is exceedingly blessed because of you.

I am inspired by your growth and development as learners, leaders, and lights!

Continue to crave the sincere milk of the Word.

For by it you will continue to grow in your salvation.

Don't let anyone look down on you because you are young, but set an example for the believers in speech, conduct, love, faith and purity.

1Timothy 4:12-NIV

ACKNOWLEDGMENTS

----❖ ❖ ❖----

I would like to first acknowledge the One who **is** my new life, living hope and eternal love--JESUS CHRIST.   I am forever grateful for the riches of His glory and the privilege and honor to serve in His name.

So many family and friends have been encouraging and supportive of me during this project. I sincerely thank you with all of my heart. My words will fail to express just how instrumental you have been in one of the most challenging and sobering seasons of my life. Each one of you has helped me endure and overcome. Thank you for praying, giving, calling, listening and sharing your wisdom.

- *Thank you, **Susanna** for reading many chapters and providing great critiques. Your friendship and input has been invaluable. The journey would not be the same without you by my side.*
- *Thank you, **Anita & Mitchell** (Parents), **Genesis & Heather** (Sisters) for reviewing my many design ideas and providing great feedback. Mom for encouraging me to continue pursuing my creative passions.*
- *Thank you, **Bolden** (Dad) for being a listening ear throughout this project and reminding me that I can do it!*
- *Thank you, **Efrem** (Brother) for sharing with me your extraordinary excitement about this project. You will not believe how that ignited a fire within me.*
- *Thank you, **Pastor Carlton Arthurs** for your spiritual leadership as founding Pastor of Wheaton Christian Center church and for giving me the honor of interviewing you for this project. Your words changed my life forever.*

- ***Thank you, Anne*** *for your devoted friendship and faithful example of God's love and compassion. Your heart for God is admirable!*
- ***Thank you, Renee*** *for all the long encouraging talks and for always sharing your heart. You are a true sister.*
- ***Thank you, Nancy*** *for being a champion of prayer and allowing me to share your powerful story in this project.*
- ***Thank you, Paula*** *for enduring hardships and blessing me and others with your pain. Your story brings healing!*
- ***Thank you, Denise*** *(Cousin) for being willing to share your feedback and incredible talents as I prepared to launch my Social Media platforms. You really saved the day!*
- ***Thank you, Women of the Moms in Prayer Group*** *(W.C.G.S.) for praying and encouraging me through the storm. Your demonstrations of love and support have been an anchor for me and my boys.*
- ***Thank you, Terri K. and Lara K.*** *for sharing with me your wealth of knowledge and experience. You helped me find my way.*
- ***Thank you, Aleah M.*** *for responding to the Lord's leading and taking on this project as editor. You are a gift from above.*

TABLE OF CONTENTS

----❖❖❖----

THE WAITING ROOM

Wisdom For Waiting Victoriously By Faith!

----------------❖❖❖----------------

Felicia E. Emanuel

----❖ ❖ ❖----

___The Waiting Room:___

"A room provided for the use of people who are waiting."-- (The Dictionary)

A season of time preceding the fulfillment of a prayer request. -- *(Felicia E. Emanuel)*

----❖ ❖ ❖----

INTRODUCTION

I am absolutely in love with the Word of God! *"Thy **words** were found, and I did eat them; and thy **word** was unto me the joy and rejoicing of mine heart: for I am called by thy name, O LORD God of hosts" (Jeremiah 15:16-KJV).* God's Word is full of wisdom, abounding with great and precious promises. One of the most familiar Biblical promises is found in the Gospel of Matthew, chapter seven: "Ask and you will receive, seek and you will find, knock and the door will be opened for you." It sounds simple, as if the process only consists of two steps: asking and receiving, or seeking and finding, or knocking and the door opening. The process, however, is much more complex. Asking, seeking or knocking, leads to a season of waiting, which I call *The Waiting Room.* This timespan precedes receiving, finding and the opened door. You may determine when you knock, but God the Father determines when the door opens. The challenge for us is being ready to enter. Readiness is dependent on the decisions you make during your time in *The Waiting Room.*

Who you are or what skills, assets or gifting you possess do not matter. At some point, you will enter *The Waiting Room.* If waiting is without question, then how you wait is of critical importance. Surprisingly, I have discovered that waiting is more challenging than working. When you are busy working, at least you know what you are doing and understand the goal. Waiting, on the other hand, introduces an uncomfortable element of uncertainty, potentially leading to frustration and a host of other unpleasant emotions.

Few people enjoy waiting. American culture is saturated with instant gratification. We live in a culture of convenience. Food, loans and services are available in an instant and with the onslaught of technology, even people. There is now an expectation to answer a person's call or respond to their text message the moment it reaches the phone. I can remember leaving the house and conducting business all day long, without a thought of needing a telephone. Today, we cannot seem to leave a room without grabbing our cell phone. These modern conveniences have made waiting increasingly difficult to practice. Yet, knowing how to wait successfully is a necessary discipline to develop. Somehow we must slow down, take a deep breath and reacquaint ourselves with the process of waiting.

If anyone needs to understand and master the process of waiting, it is those called to live by faith. Living by faith is a supernatural lifestyle that consists of multiple lessons *in waiting*. The next time you turn to Matthew 7:7 try reading it like this: "Ask, *then wait* and you will receive, seek, *then wait* and you will find, knock, *then wait* and the door will be opened." Believers need to possess God's wisdom to wait. Believers cannot afford to be hasty or unwise. Often-times circumstances can appear to be one way, but, in reality, are not the way they appear. Do not make conclusions based on sight alone. Your problem may appear, in the natural sight, to not be working out, but when you look at it with the eyes of faith you may see something completely different. As you read prepare to receive God's wisdom for your *Waiting Room* and keep in mind that it is through faith and patience that we inherit God's promises *(Hebrews 6:12).*

During a major time of transition in my life the Lord began to speak to me about the need of wisdom for waiting. Honestly, it never occurred to me that I needed wisdom to wait. In my mind, waiting required nothing more than showing up and letting time pass, knowing that whatever I was waiting for would happen at the appointed time. Instead, the Lord showed me that waiting in the natural realm was not the same as waiting in the spiritual realm. In the natural realm waiting can be an inactive process, but the spiritual realm requires engagement. We must remain sober and vigilant at all times because our adversary, the devil, is roaming around like a roaring lion seeking whom he can devour *(1 Peter 5:8)*. We cannot afford to become complacent while waiting for our desires to be fulfilled. *The Waiting Room* is not a safety-zone, but remains a part of the war-zone. It may sound cozy and quiet, but, on the contrary, it is hazardous and fair ground to be engaged in battle. Sadly, many people have lost the good fight while in *The Waiting Room* due to letting down their guard to the unexpected, subtle attacks of the enemy.

God's wisdom provides the strategy for victory in obtaining the promise. Believe me, the enemy is using an organized strategy to tempt you to abandon your hopes and desires while you wait. His plan is to always deceive you into aborting your hope in the promise so that it will never come to pass. God's will is that you use His great wisdom as your strategy of defense. I was amazed as the Lord began exposing the enemy's common strategies to distract and discourage us and how applying His wisdom would defeat the enemy's plans every time. It became clear I needed to change my approach from constantly praying about my desires to seeking God for His wisdom that would ensure a victorious *Waiting Room* experience.

My Journey Begins:

After being laid off from my job with a major mobile phone manufacturer, I sensed it was time for me to pursue the passion of my heart. I no longer desired to work in Corporate America. I longed to work in the areas of my passions and purpose. I felt that it was now my chance to pursue my heart's desire: creating music. I love music. I love singing. I love writing inspirational words in the form of poems and songs. All I wanted now was an opportunity to use my passion for music and creative writing professionally. I believed that the Lord was leading me to do just that. I started seeking God for direction and an opened door. My prayers were specific and comprehensive. "Lord, show me how to gain access into the music industry. I want to be a Contemporary Inspirational Recording Artist. I want my songs to be played on the radio, in movies, commercials and plays." I began declaring and standing on the Word of God: *"A man's gift makes room for him and brings him before great men" (Proverbs 18:16-KJV)* and *"I will praise the name of God with a song, and magnify Him with thanksgiving" (Psalm 69:30-KJV).* I was excited when the Lord spoke to my heart from 2 Chronicles 15:7, *"Be ye strong therefore and let not your hands be weak; for your work shall be rewarded"* (KJV). Little did I know that I would need this word to anchor and encourage me throughout the *Waiting Room* experience!

My faith was strong. I felt excited and hopeful. Thoughts of "I can do this" and "this is the right time" filled my head. It has been my long-awaited dream to record my original songs and release an album. I was anxious to begin putting action behind what I believed. However, I did not know the first thing about recording a CD. I turned to the place most of us turn to today for information: the Internet. I researched the music business, how to produce and budget for an independent music project, and anything else that could help me prepare. I was able to find a lot of helpful information, but what I really wanted was an opportunity to learn from someone in the music business. Surprisingly, I was given that opportunity--so I thought.

A friend worked with a woman whose client was an established Gospel Artist. He asked if she would connect me with the artist so I could get a close up look at the music industry and gain experience working on one of his projects. Incredibly he agreed and initially set up a lunch appointment with me and his music producer. I was elated, to say the least, but soon the appointment changed from lunch to me visiting his church office to meet with him and his staff. I was fine with that, willing to do whatever it took to get me closer to my passion and dream. Updated resume in hand, and a very professional look, I entered the church office ahead of time to make a great impression. During the meeting he shared that his team had recently completed a great project that I could have worked on, but he would consider me for a future one. Although I was not happy about missing an opportunity, I was thrilled that he was willing to give me a chance. He came across as a really down-to-earth and overall nice guy. I was surprised he shared his thoughts so unguardedly, which made me feel welcomed as if I was already part of the team.

The atmosphere of the meeting changed after he noticed on my resume that I had a professional background in television production. He shared that his church was building a new facility and needed consultation setting up their media area. He asked if I would be interested in helping. This caught me completely off guard. I was here because I needed something; I had not expected to be needed. Thinking back, maybe my reaction was questionable because, although I agreed to help out in any way I could, I was clearly not interested in revisiting my past production life. I had been away from that type of work for over six years and felt that my skills were out of date, but I did not want to throw away the opportunity or appear ungrateful. I tried to answer all his production related questions intelligently. I am not certain if I achieved any impression with my outdated knowledge, but I tried my best. He picked up on my uneasiness and simply stated that he would help me, even if I did not help them. I, again, assured him that I was willing to do whatever I could. Perhaps I was not convincing enough, or maybe he was not convinced that I knew enough.

Before the meeting ended I asked if he would critique a few of my songs. He agreed and warned me that he would be completely honest. I told him I could take it, but left with mixed feelings. Did I mess things up by not being current in my field? Would he follow through and call me when he begins a new project? I made sure I followed through. I purchased a voice recorder, sang three of my songs, and sent them to his producer for feedback. It took a long time for him to comment and the verdict was simply: *nice songs but not commercial.* I never received a call to work on any projects or to advise on the church's media needs.

From the time I left that meeting, I have battled the enemy's voice suggesting I was not good enough. I was not good enough to advise on their media needs, work on their music projects or record my own music. It took everything I knew to resist this lie and stand firm on the truth. The truth is God determines my worth and everything God has given me has value. *"Every good and perfect gift is from above, coming down from the Father of the heavenly lights, who does not change like shifting shadows" (James1:17-KJV).* In reality, I am the only one "good enough" to fulfill God's will and plan for me.

I have experienced a number of disappointments and delays on my recording journey. Honestly, I did not expect to experience much opposition. When I began I was under the impression that the most difficult part would be meeting the budget, and then everything else would easily fall into place. I soon discovered just how wrong I was. I had the money and the songs, but could not secure the skilled professionals who were right to work on the project. The excitement over my initial progress was gone and I was confused. Why did promising doors close and nothing work out? If God is with me and what I am doing is His will, why would there be such opposition?

It was in this place of confusion that I received the revelation of applying God's wisdom as I waited for the fulfillment of my desires. That was the day *The Waiting Room* concept was born and the need to write this book was put in my heart. I am still in *The Waiting Room* and, although it has not been an easy process, I am committed to continuing the work and completing the journey. Despite the challenges, I believe that one day all the right doors will open and I will successfully produce, record, and release a music project. I believe one day my name and picture will be found on the cover of a great contemporary inspirational music CD.

Over the next eleven chapters I invite you to join me on an amazing journey of gaining God's wisdom for your *Waiting Room*. You may find yourself in *The Waiting Room* for promotion, direction, healing in your body, a child or a spouse. Whatever the specific need, God's wisdom is required. Oftentimes hopes and desires are abandoned in *The Waiting Room* simply because this place is difficult. Especially when time continues to pass and life continues to change. Seemingly everything is changing except the thing you are waiting for. You grow older. Your symptoms worsen. Other people continue to be promoted over you. Another friend gets married. Your heart may be filled with questions of why: Why am I still single? Why am I childless? Why am I not more successful? Why do I have a gift and no platform? Why? Why? Why?

I assure you, God has an answer. Just like you I, too, have been desperate for my waiting to come to an end. Yet, more importantly, I now realize it is better to focus on applying God's wisdom while I wait than to be consumed with when the waiting will end. God will take care of that part. He is faithful. The door is going to open. Your answer will come. Your desire will come to pass. If you apply God's wisdom in *The Waiting Room*, He will surely bring your waiting to a victorious end.

2

MAKE RIGHT DECISIONS

There is a way which seems right to a man, but in the end it leads to death (Proverbs 14:12 – WEB).

I do not know who originated the saying: "your life is the sum total of the decisions you make", but I believe it. Decisions have powerful implications. Thousands of decisions are made daily. What is the likelihood that some of those decisions will be wrong? Would it be the same likelihood that some of those decisions will be right? The determining factor whether the decisions will be right or wrong lies in the mind. Decisions are the fruit of thoughts, and thoughts are directly connected to living. Perhaps a better way to say it is: "where the mind goes, the man follows".

Negative, fearful or bitter thoughts multiply, resulting in an abundance of those characteristics in life. Those characteristics are the seeds that foster the kind of thoughts that lead to wrong decisions. My heart broke as I listened to a nearly forty year old believer explain her decision to have sex with her boyfriend on the foundation that she did not want to be like the character in the movie "The Forty-Year-Old Virgin." She had preserved herself for 39.9 years and due to the influence of a Hollywood movie she decided to stop waiting. I remember wondering how something like this could happen. Does the media possess such great of power and influence over minds? She later shared her regret over her decision. After a few years she met, fell in love, and married her soulmate.

The decisions made in *The Waiting Room* can be carried with us into the next chapters of our lives. People make tragic decisions daily based on corrupt and defiled thinking patterns of this world. To avoid succumbing to these patterns the mind cannot be conformed to their way of thinking. Romans 12:2 reveals the key: *"Do not conform to the pattern of this world, but be transformed by the renewing of your mind. Then you will be able to test and approve what God's will is—His good, pleasing, and perfect will" (NIV)*. The first step to right decision making is to have a renewed mind. Renew means to reestablish or resume after an interruption. Our thoughts are to be in alignment with God's thoughts. If the mind is aligned with the world's way of thinking, then the connection to God's way of thinking is broken. The connection must then be reestablished by allowing the Holy Spirit to renew your mind through God's Word. *"Throw off your old sinful nature and your former way of life, which is corrupted by lust and deception. Instead, let the Spirit renew your thoughts and attitudes" (Ephesians 4:23-NLT)*. When our minds have been changed or renewed by the Word of God, we will think like God. His attitudes become our attitudes. His passion becomes our passion. His purpose becomes our purpose. A new pattern of thinking is established and the old way of thinking according to the world's patterns is no longer a frame of reference. The more time spent exposed to the Word of God results in thinking more like Him.

Focus is also influential in the decision making process. After the mind has been renewed by the Word of God, focus on the truth is maintained by allowing the Spirit of Truth to lead in every aspect of life. Sometimes it is necessary to reevaluate and readjust focus. There is a tendency to zoom in on one area of irritation or struggle, causing it to appear larger than it is. A word of wisdom I often encourage myself with when my focus becomes off is: *Do not allow the one percent to overshadow the ninety-nine.* Focusing only on the one percent of things that are going wrong in life will overshadow the ninety-nine percent of things that are going right. Pull back to bring that area into proper perspective. You may find it was never as bad as it appeared when it was the only thing in view.

You may not possess every desire of your heart, but take an intentional inventory of what you do have and never dismiss any gain. Satan cannot be allowed to deceive the way he deceived Eve in the garden. Do not fall for the lie that you are missing out by not experiencing what you desire. Consider Eve's outcome and be warned. Choose to obey God and receive your desire His way. God will not withhold any good thing from you. It is His good pleasure to bless your life with every kind of blessing. Trust His wisdom to receive your desires according to His will because Satan seeks to exploit and seduce you into sin. Do not take a bite of the forbidden fruit! Resist the devil and submit to God by doing what His Word says and the devil will flee from you *(James 4:7)*.

My Waiting Room Lesson:

I have personally experienced how a loss of focus can result from wrong decisions. It was during, what was supposed to be one of the happiest times in my life, that my husband and I purchased our first house. As first-time buyers we were excited to be purchasing a new construction. We chose the final finishings, colors and configurations. Our first child was under two and I was eight months pregnant with our second when we moved in. My husband worked full-time in the transportation industry to support us and I stayed home with our children and managed the household.

Of course I wanted to decorate our brand new place right away. The white walls needed color; every window needed some type of covering, and a few rooms needed furniture. We were financially challenged, living paycheck to paycheck with little savings. Our cars were paid off and only six hundred dollars in credit card debt. We had no other debt, and planned to keep it that way, until one day my husband decided to buy a new car. In my mind there was absolutely nothing wrong with his car, and if there was a problem he had the skills to fix it. I think he was tired of driving an old, beat-up looking car. To entice me into agreement with his decision he offered me a deal. If he could get a new car, I could get new furniture and decorate the house.

I knew better, but in that moment I did not want him to get what he wanted and I get nothing. The feeling of not wanting to be left out and the temptation of no interest, no payments for a year financing was strong. He traded-in his car for a newer one and I filled nearly every room in our house with new furniture.

I started in the Master bedroom with a new bedroom set and couch, chair, ottoman and table for the sitting room. Then, a new bunk bed set for our son's room. This was followed by a new dining room set, couch, chair and ottoman for the living room. Mirrors for the walls, new hanging lamp and gold fixtures for the half bathroom as the silver fixtures did not match my décor. I ordered custom blinds for all the windows, painted every room and added crown molding around the two-level dining area. Finally, I bought new pillows, comforters, sheets, towels, throws, pictures, and any other cute little doo-dad my heart desired

Our house was beautiful, but our finances became an ugly mess. The initial six hundred dollars of debt had increased to around thirty thousand dollars (including the car). We never paid off any of the bills before the 12 months of no interest, no payments for a year ended. Our bills steadily increased to the point we rarely had cash left to purchase food and gas. We fell into an endless cycle of credit card dependency attempting to get from one paycheck to the next.

A few years of living in financial bondage we accepted the sad reality that we could no longer afford to live in our beautifully decorated house and put it on the market. Our beautiful decorative touches stayed with the house, but the thousands of dollars of debt followed us to a cramped two bedroom apartment.

I lamented the loss of our house for months. Not only was I disappointed and ashamed, but I was mad, too. I was not mad at God, but did hold some resentment toward my husband for making the deal. However, I was mostly mad at myself. I made the decisions that led to the demise of a dream. I chose to give into temptation and in the process made a number of wrong decisions. I made the choices that plunged us into thousands of dollars of debt. There is a thin line between faith and presumption, and I discovered I had acted out of the latter. It was presumptuous to assume that God providing a new house meant He would also provide the means to pay for everything I desired to purchase for it. What I should have done was to seek the Lord for the things I desired for the house and waited until He provided the means for me to act.

After four years in our apartment we purchased another new construction property and, believe me, I remembered the lessons of our first house! I wanted to paint the boring white walls and buy some new furniture, but I chose to maintain my focus and wait until the Lord provided. I vowed to not accumulate any new debt and to operate on a cash-only basis. It was freeing to buy things with cash or charge them and pay-off the bill every month. I could actually say I owned the things I purchased. Unfortunately, I never got to paint or decorate that house because four years later we ended up selling it in a short-sale. My lesson was tough, but out of it came something good: a renewed mind and a determination to make right decision in *The Waiting Room*.

David's Waiting Room To The Throne:

King David is a great example of someone who made right decisions in *The Waiting Room*. His *Waiting Room* for the throne was a long, challenging and eventful experience. Yet, somehow, he was able to keep his focus and the hardships of his life in the proper perspective.

The youngest of eight brothers, David took care of the family sheep. The book of First Samuel tells how he protected those sheep with a heart that God admired. God was with David in the fields and gave David the strength to defeat any enemy that attacked or threated his area of responsibility. He killed a lion and a bear with his bare hands. He was fearless and courageous.

Saul, the current King of Israel, had been rejected by God for his disobedience. The Prophet Samuel was sent to the house of Jesse in Bethlehem, for God had chosen one of his sons to be the new king. Out of all eight of Jesse's sons, some tall, strong and handsome, David, the youngest brother, was chosen and anointed king over Israel. From that point God took David out of the fields and placed him in the forefront of the nation of Israel. He became the anointed Psalmist who relieved King Saul when tormented by an evil spirit. He gained notoriety and wealth after killing the Philistine champion Goliath. He successfully led Israel's army to many victories over their enemies.

David's journey consisted of many highs and just as many lows. His success and obvious favor from the Lord was bitterly envied by King Saul, who persecuted him and tried to kill him at every opportunity. David spent many years of his life on the run from this rejected ruler. Yet, in spite of his great troubles, the Bible says that David behaved wisely. He did not allow his suffering to provoke him into making a wrong decision. That would have frustrated the purpose of God in him becoming King.

Although King Saul never stopped pursuing David with the intent to kill him, David never raised his hand to harm King Saul. He was wise and knew not to touch God's anointed. He chose to allow the One who put Saul in office to remove him from office. As a result of King David applying God's wisdom and making right decisions, look what God declared concerning him: *"Now then, tell my servant, David, this is what the LORD Almighty says: I took you from the pasture, from tending the flock, and appointed you ruler over my people Israel. I have been with you wherever you have gone, and I have cut off all your enemies from before you. Now I will make your name great, like the names of the greatest men on earth. And I will provide a place for my people Israel and will plant them so that they can have a home of their own and no longer be disturbed. Wicked people will not oppress them anymore, as they did at the beginning and have done ever since the time I appointed leaders over my people Israel. I will also give you rest from all your enemies. "The LORD declares to you that the LORD himself will establish a house for you: When your days are over and you rest with your ancestors, I will raise up your offspring to succeed you, your own flesh and blood, and I will establish his kingdom. He is the one who will build a house for my Name, and I will establish the throne of his kingdom forever. I will be his father, and he will be my son. When he does wrong, I will punish him with a rod wielded by men, with floggings inflicted by human hands. But my love will never be taken away from him, as I took it away from Saul, whom I removed from before you. Your house and your kingdom will endure forever before me; your throne will be established forever"* (2 Samuel 7:8-16-NIV).

I do not think David would have received such a great blessing had he responded inappropriately in his test and made decisions outside God's will. His story would read differently had he took it upon himself to relieve his frustration and source of suffering. Perhaps you are in a similar situation as King David; on your way to

15

promotion and prosperity, but plagued with conflict and strife. "This is what the Lord says to you, do not be afraid or dismayed because of this great multitude, for the battle is not yours, but God's" (2 Chronicles 20:15-NKJV). God will fight every battle and bring you into the promise as you honor Him while you wait.

Abraham's Waiting Room To An Heir:

Do you remember Abraham and Sarah's *Waiting Room* experience? In Genesis Chapter 15, Abraham expressed to the Lord his concern in not having a natural born heir. Eleazar, his faithful servant, would be left as steward over all his possessions. The Lord assures Abraham that Eleazar would not become his heir, but he would have a natural born son to inherit all his possessions.

It took time for the promise to be fulfilled and as they waited Sarah became discouraged and made a few wrong decisions. First, she makes an erroneous conclusion that the Lord was keeping her from bearing a child. Then, she makes a wrong decision to give Abraham her Egyptian handmaid Hagar to bear children for her. Although this decision did result in the birth of a son, Ishmael, it also birthed a host of negative consequences. Many of these consequences even have influence in the present.

In Genesis, chapter 21, Sarah conceives and gives birth to a son named Isaac. The very desire for which Abraham prayed and they waited, came to pass. The Lord was faithful to perform His promise. Unfortunately, some of the decisions that they made while in *The Waiting Room*, cast a dark shadow over their blessing.

The lesson from Abraham and Sarah's situation is summed up in Romans 15:4. *"Such things were written in the scriptures long ago to teach us. And the scriptures give us hope and encouragement as we wait patiently for God's promises to be fulfilled" (NLT).* It really does not matter whose story I tell. My story,

King David's, Abraham and Sarah's or yours: the reality is that we all have the same human nature including a proclivity to error and a potential to sin. We all need constant renewing through the Word of God. We all need to maintain our focus on Truth and allow the Spirit of Truth to lead in everything that pertains to the new life.

Determine in your heart today to make right decisions as you wait on the Lord to fulfill His promises in your life. Have the mind of Christ. Think the thoughts of God and keep the journey of your life in the right perspective. You may feel you cannot make it another day in your current circumstance, but recognize how far you have come with God's grace and trust His grace will prove sufficient for the rest of the wait.

3

MAINTAIN READINESS

Therefore, my beloved brethren, be steadfast, immovable, always abounding in the work of the Lord, knowing that your labor is not in vain in the Lord (1 Corinthians 15:58-NKJV).

Getting ready for success and staying ready for success are two distinctly different things. That was the lesson the five foolish virgins learned while waiting for the bridegroom: *"Then the kingdom of heaven shall be likened to ten virgins who took their lamps and went out to meet the bridegroom. Now five of them were wise, and five were foolish. Those who were foolish took their lamps and took no oil with them, but the wise took oil in their vessels with their lamps. But while the bridegroom was delayed, they all slumbered and slept. And at midnight a cry was heard: 'Behold, the bridegroom is coming, go out to meet him!' Then all those virgins arose and trimmed their lamps. And the foolish said to the wise, 'Give us some of your oil, for our lamps are going out.' But the wise answered, saying, 'No, lest there should not be enough for us and you; but go rather to those who sell, and buy for yourselves.' And while they went to buy, the bridegroom came, and those who were ready went in with him to the wedding; and the door was shut. Afterward the other virgins came also, saying, 'Lord, Lord, open to us!' But he answered and said, 'Assuredly, I say to you, I do not know you.' Watch therefore, for you know neither the day nor the hour in which the Son of Man is coming"* (Matthew 25:1-13-NKJV).

It is impossible to determine the length of time that will be spent in *The Waiting Room*. The longer the wait, the more temptation there is to lose focus or lose heart. No matter how challenging, it is essential to maintain readiness throughout the waiting period. Readiness is the state of being fully prepared for something and the willingness to do something. Understanding the requirements and exercising discipline will help you stay prepared. In the previous parable, the five foolish virgins lose their focus and fail to maintain their readiness. All the virgins had oil lamps to provide them with light for seeing and joining the bridegroom and his wedding party upon arrival. Apparently, the five foolish virgins thought that the wedding party would arrive in a short duration of time. They did not find it necessary to bring any extra oil, because they assumed the oil in their lamps would prove sufficient for the waiting period. Their assumptions result in the loss of their rewards. No one wants to suffer loss. Life in Christ is like a treasure hunt and at the end of every *Waiting Room* experience is a blessing of great value to find. Be like the five wise virgins: understand the goal, be disciplined and stay committed to the end to receive your reward.

Salaam's Readiness Story:

As a picture of maintaining readiness in *The Waiting Room*, imagine the lifestyle of an athlete. Any athlete who aspires to be proficient in a sport, especially on a professional level, must maintain their readiness at all times. Performance and success require a great deal of discipline. It does not matter whether the season is on or off, athletes must maintain their readiness physically, mentally and socially. Professional athletes are held accountable to a personal conduct and disciplinary policy. These policies outline expectations on alcohol, tobacco and drug uses, as well as any violent and criminal behaviors. If an athlete violates any of the policies, they may face fines and or suspensions.

Playing sports professionally is a highly competitive and demanding commitment. Athletes must realize that the same diligence that prepares them to perform is also required to maintain their performance. The career of Heisman Trophy winner Rashaan Salaam provides an example of what can happen when readiness is not maintained. In 1994 Salaam achieved as a running back one of the best collegiate seasons ever recorded at the University of Colorado. He obtained 2,055 rushing yards and 24 touchdowns. The Chicago Bears drafted him the following year as the 21st pick in the first round. His rookie season was moderately successful with him rushing for over 1,000 yards. After that point, though, things started going downhill. By 2000, he was completely out of the NFL. In 2001, he resurfaced with the Memphis Manix in the XFL, but his professional playing career eventually ended in 2004, after being suspended by the Toronto Argonauts in the CFL.

Salaam's interview with the ESPN program "Outside the Lines" provides helpful insight into what went wrong. In the interview, Salaam spoke candidly about some of the tragic mistakes he made during his career. He was quoted as saying: "I didn't realize coming up how much work you had to put in once you got to the NFL." Salaam goes on to share how marijuana contributed to his poor performance and disappointing career. He said, "Marijuana makes you lazy, makes you not want to get up and work out," and, "I had all the talent in the world, you know, great body, great genes, but I had no work ethic and I had no discipline." He now realizes, "The better you get, the harder you have to work," but instead, "The better I got, the lazier I got." Salaam came to realize that being an incredible, natural athlete was not enough to succeed. Unfortunately, he figured that out too late - after his NFL career was over. Salaam was on his way to achieving NFL success, but failed to maintain the readiness required to achieve it. I respect Salaam's honesty in sharing his failures and, hopefully, his story can help others avoid making the same mistakes.

My Readiness Story:

This reminds me of the time during which my husband and I were selling our first house. Though we had not received an offer, we still had to keep our house clean, organized and ready to be shown. After each showing, we hoped and prayed this would be the day we received an offer. I was especially invested since I was the main person cleaning and preparing the house for the next showing! I had to maintain readiness for the potential buyer. Every day I would pick up the kids' toys and freshen up the bathrooms because potential buyers would see our For-Sale sign and sometimes stop by without an appointment. Had I stopped cleaning and keeping things organized we might not have attracted our buyer.

I will never forget the day the lady who eventually bought our house came by. It was late in the evening and I had just started cooking dinner when the telephone rang. It was a realtor asking if her client could come in and see our property. Her client had been driving around our neighborhood and saw our For-Sale-By-Owner sign in the front yard. Since it had not been long since our last showing, we agreed.

From the moment I opened the front door to let her in the showing became magical. Her eyes dazzled as she took in every detail of the tour. She loved everything. She loved the paint on the walls, the two-story dining area and upon seeing the master bedroom the deal was sealed. I think it was the sitting area in our huge bedroom that did it. She could see herself relaxing and enjoying this space. It was clear that this was the property she desired to buy and, before the night was over, she had her realtor call with an offer. Maintaining our readiness paid off big time. All the constant cleaning and keeping things organized was beneficial in the end. We achieved what we had been waiting for, resulting in a successful *Waiting Room* experience.

Ruth's Readiness Story:

The book of Ruth contains a beautiful and encouraging example of maintaining readiness. Ruth details an exciting and elaborate account of a Moabite woman inheriting a good future from the Israelite God, Jehovah. Due to a famine in Israel, the Hebrew family of Elimelech moved from Bethlehem-Judah to Moab. Elimelech and his wife Naomi had two sons, Mahlon and Chilion. Each of them married Moabite women. After some time Elimelech and his sons die, leaving Naomi and her daughter-in-laws widows.

After the death of her husband and sons, Naomi decides to return to her country. She heard while in Moab that the famine was over. She and her daughter-in-laws proceeded to travel to Judah. During the journey, Naomi tells them to return to their mothers' houses. She blessed them saying *"May the Lord deal kindly with you as you have dealt with the dead and with me; the Lord grant you rest in the house of your husband" (Ruth 1:8-9-KJV)*. However, through many tears, they begged to go with her. After explaining that she was unable to provide them with new husbands, Orpah turned back, but Ruth clung to her determined to go. Ruth said, *"Entreat me not to leave you, or to turn back from following after you; for wherever you go, I will go; and wherever you lodge, I will lodge; your people shall be my people, and your God my God. Where you die, I will die, and there will I be buried. The Lord do so to me and more also, if anything but death parts you and me" (Ruth 1:16-17-JKV)*. Thus, Naomi and Ruth returned together to Judah.

Ruth could have returned to her mother's house. She shared the desire of being remarried like her sister-in-law Orpah, who chose to reclaim her pagan family, traditions and god. Orpah concluded that her future held more promise in her own country, trusting in familiar paganism rather than a foreign country and a foreign God. Ruth, on the other hand, must have had an encounter with the True and Living God in her land. Her Hebrew worship encounter made a deep impact in order for Ruth to walk away and leave what was familiar behind. Ruth was persuaded that the God of the Hebrews would do good and bless her with a good future.

As Naomi and Ruth entered the town of Bethlehem, Ruth's *Waiting Room* experience begins to unfold. Naomi's late-husband Elimelech had a wealthy relative. He was a rich farmer named Boaz. In order to provide for herself and Naomi Ruth would work in his field gleaning crops behind the reapers. The custom of the land was to not harvest the corners of the fields in addition to the crops dropped by the reapers for the poor, widows, orphans and strangers to collect. Ruth found favor with Boaz because of her loyalty to Naomi. He heard of all she did in caring for her aged mother-in-law. Boaz instructed Ruth to only glean in his field under his protection. He provided food when she was hungry and water when she was thirsty. He instructed his reapers to purposely drop crops for Ruth to glean. She collected so much that Naomi was prompted to ask where she had been gleaning. When Naomi heard it was the field of her close relative Boaz, she was greatly encouraged.

Naomi said to Ruth, "My daughter, shall I not seek security for you; that it may be well with you?" Naomi instructs Ruth on what to do to secure a good future. She tells Ruth to wash, put on perfume and her best attire, and sneak down to the threshing floor where Boaz would be working that night. Naomi cautioned Ruth to remain hidden until Boaz finished eating and drinking and lay down.

After he fell asleep she was to uncover his feet and lay down there. Ruth did everything Naomi instructed.

As a result, Boaz and Ruth married and she inherits a great future. By maintaining her readiness in *The Waiting Room*, Ruth was no longer looked upon as a pagan foreigner from Moab who tragically lost her husband. She was no longer looked upon as an impoverished daughter-in-law struggling to make ends meet for her and her aged mother-in-law. Now, Ruth is the wife of one of the richest men in Judah. The very field that she had sweat and labored gleaning, now belonged to her. The reapers that once threw her extra barley are now her servants. However, all this is not half of the blessing that God bestowed upon Ruth. Ruth would give birth to a son named Obed. Obed was the father of Jesse, who was the father of King David. The greatest miracle for this pagan girl from Moab is that she ends up being a part of the lineage of Jesus Christ. The Savior of the world, the Redeemer came through her seed. God brought a fruitful end to a journey that began with famine, death and great loss.

Whatever you desire to accomplish in your life, know that anything worthwhile requires discipline. You have to be willing to work hard and keep working hard until your goals are accomplished. *"Let's not get tired of doing what is good, for at the right time we will reap a harvest—if we do not give up (Galatians 6:9-ISV).* Stay committed to the work that is required for success. Success is achieved on purpose. When blessed with an opportunity, do not take it for granted. Seek wise counsel, develop a plan, perfect skills and keep exercising faith until the intended goal is established.

If by chance you lose focus and get off track, don't lose hope! You can always decide to get back on track. Simply begin again. Be determined that you are going to achieve your goals and enjoy the fruit of your labor. Be certain of His will for your life. God has appointed you to succeed and has ordained a good future for you. Make sure not to fall short of the grace he has provided. *"Knowing that the proving of your faith works endurance, but let endurance have its perfect work in you, that you may be perfect and complete, lacking in nothing" (James 1:3-4-WEB).*

4

DENY DISCOURAGEMENT

I have told you these things, so that in me you may have peace. In this world you will have trouble. But take heart! I have overcome the world (John 16:33-NIV).

It is not uncommon to begin *The Waiting Room* experience feeling encouraged and optimistic one day, then fearful and discouraged the next. One of the main spirits encountered in *The Waiting Room* is the spirit of discouragement. The temptation to worry about life, what you will eat, wear and experience often comes to defeat your faith in the One who promises to faithfully supply everything you need.

Discouragement is the act of making something less likely to happen or a feeling of having lost hope or confidence. Discouragement desires to hinder us from achieving goals by robbing confidence and hope. The process of beginning encouraged and ending up discouraged is through losing heart. The surest way to lose heart is by making assumptions based on what can or cannot be seen. Believers are called to live by faith and not by sight. If overwhelmed by anything in life, we must pray and trust God to help—and He will. *"God is able to do immeasurably more than all we ask or imagine, according to His power that is at work within us" (Ephesians 3:20-NIV).* Despite uncertainty, God will supply His power to overcome discouragement and endure with His peace.

It is an advantage to understand that discouragement is a choice! It is a choice to be discouraged, not an automatic response. Permission must be granted to feel discouraged. Circumstances do not determine encouragement or discouragement, but choices. *God said "I call heaven and earth to testify against you today! I've set life and death before you today: both blessings and curses. Choose life, that it may be well with you—you and your children"* *(Deuteronomy 30:19-ISV).* There is always a choice to be made. It is clear God strongly encourages choosing life, not death. Yet, in every circumstance, we are free to exercise our will. The ability to choose is one of the most powerful God-given rights we possess. It is the determining factor for success or failure. Circumstances can be faced in the power of encouragement or in the defeat of discouragement. This decision will make the difference.

I recall an occasion where I struggled with discouragement because I chose to believe the lie that I was limited by my own efforts and resources. God had revealed to me some wonderful things He planned to do in my life. Initially I was excited as I sensed His leading and discerned His hand working on my behalf. Everything appeared to be coming together, but, suddenly, I experienced a shifting and nothing I thought God was working in appeared to work out. I then began entertaining thoughts of discouragement. I lost heart and doubted everything of which I was once sure. Only by returning to the initial promises of God and accepting them as the truth was I able to defeat and deny discouragement.

The correct response to the lies of the spirit of discouragement is to counter them with the truth of God's Word. The Word of God can always be trusted. If God spoke it, shall He not perform it? God spoke to Joshua, *"Have I not commanded you? Be strong and courageous. Do not be afraid; do not be discouraged, for the LORD your God will be with you wherever you* go" *(Joshua 1:9-NIV)*. The Lord is near in the times of peace and in the times of trouble. Therefore, be strong and courageous! Do not be frightened or dismayed. Everything the Lord has commanded can be done. Accept His words as true and let nothing convince you otherwise. When discouragement comes, deny it. Deny it a voice. Deny it any recognition or regard. Deny it access to your mind or a place in your heart. The voice that speaks contrary to what God said to you must be rejected. *"So place yourselves under God's authority. Resist the devil, and he will run away from you"* *(James 4:7-GWT)*.

Rest assured that when God leads the action, He does not abandon it. Even though there may be times when His presence is not felt or discerning what He is doing is difficult, continue to believe and know He is faithful and will see us through to the completion of His will. Only quitting assures failure. Whatever happens, do not give up. It is common to feel weak at times, but feeling weak is no reason to quit. God promises to renew strength. *Have you not known? Have you not heard? That the Everlasting God, the Lord, the Creator of the ends of the earth, neither faints nor is weary? There is no searching of His understanding. He gives power to the faint, and to them that have no might, He increases strength (Isaiah 40:28-29-ESV).* You can never know exactly, what is at risk, if you quit and succumb to discouragement.

Stories of Defeating Discouragement:

Just think if Beethoven had given up after his music teacher told him that as a composer he was hopeless. Today he is widely considered the greatest classical composer of all time. He wrote many of his compositions after he became deaf and his music stands as a monument to human creativity and excellence.

Thomas Edison was told by a teacher that he was too stupid to learn anything. He is considered one of the most prolific inventors in history. He held over a thousand patents and his inventions included the electric light bulb, electric generator, sound microphone and phonograph, just to name a few.

Walt Disney was fired from a newspaper because they thought he lacked imagination and had no original ideas. He pioneered new ideas in the motion picture and theme park industries. He was the first man to create a feature length movie using cell animation. He produced many classic Disney films and created today's largest entertainment company that has entertained more than 200 million people, including presidents, kings and queens, and royalty from all over the globe.

Michael Jordan encountered discouragement when he was cut from his high school basketball team. Today he is considered the greatest professional basketball player of all time. He won 6 NBA championships, earned 5 MVP awards and played in 14 All-Star games. He won 10 scoring titles and finished his career with 32,292 points, 5,633 assists and 6,672 rebounds.

If any one of these profound individuals had succumbed to discouragement history as we know it would read much differently. What you can take away from their impressive achievements is to never allow discouraging people or experiences to cause you to deny fulfilling your destiny. No matter who does not believe in you, always believe in yourself. Success can and will be achieved if you are determined to deny discouragement the power to detain, derail or destroy your drive and confidence.

Nehemiah's Story:

The spirit of discouragement and the spirit of fear operate as a team. Their two main weapons are frustration and intimidation. When I think about denying discouragement one Bible story in particular comes to mind. The book of Nehemiah details an inspirational account of how one man denied discouragement and as a result experienced great success. Nehemiah was among the Hebrews who remained in the Persian Empire following the seventy years of Babylonian captivity. King Cyrus had allowed the Israelites to return to their homeland, Jerusalem, but many remained in Persia; possibly due to their roles in the Persian government. Nehemiah was one such individual. As a high ranking official in the Persian Empire of King Artaxerxes I, one of his roles was royal cupbearer. The function of the cupbearer was to taste and serve wine to his master. Nehemiah had to ensure the quality and safety of the wine before the King drank any.

On one particular day, Nehemiah appeared to be sad in the presence of the King. The King inquired why he looked so sad. He responded that he was troubled about the news he heard from one of his countrymen: his hometown was in ruins and the people were in great distress. The walls of the city were broken down and the gates had been burned. Now, it is important to note that Nehemiah had been praying and fasting since he heard the troubling news. He was prepared to answer when the King asked how he could help. Nehemiah requested a leave of absence to go rebuild the city and the walls, letters signed by the King to ensure his safe passage through other lands, and timber from the King's forest to rebuild the walls and gates of Jerusalem. Nehemiah was granted the King's permission and all that he requested.

Not everyone in the region was happy about the fact that Nehemiah sought the well-being of the Children of Israel. Especially Sanballat the Horonite and Tobiah the Ammonite official; they were deeply disturbed. These men, along with Geshem the Arabian; attempted on several occasions to discourage the people and stop their efforts. Many times the people became discouraged and wanted to give up, but God strengthened Nehemiah and the people and they were able to deny discouragement and continue. Many of the same tactics that the enemy used to oppose Nehemiah and the people are used to oppose us today. We can learn a lot from their experience by examining exactly how the enemy attempted to discourage them.

The enemy's first attempt to discourage the people was to use mocking and ridicule. *"But it so happened, when Sanballat heard that we were rebuilding the wall, that he was furious and very indignant, and mocked the Jews. And he spoke before his brethren and the army of Samaria, and said, "What are these feeble Jews doing? Will they fortify themselves? Will they offer sacrifices? Will they complete it in a day? Will they revive the stones from the heaps of rubbish—stones that are burned?" Now Tobiah the Ammonite was beside him, and he said, "Whatever they build, if even a fox goes up on it, he will break down their stone wall"* (Nehemiah 4:1-3-NKJV).

There is an old adage that says, "Sticks and stones may break my bones but words will never hurt me." I emphatically disagree with whoever wrote this quote. Words are powerful and their impact can be devastating. No one enjoys being put down or criticized. You have to be careful not to entertain or accept what I call *verbal bullying*. People like Tobiah and Sanballat go around and try to bully others because they themselves feel weak and insecure. It could be that they are threatened by who you are or what you are pursuing. Nevertheless, you must not take on the attributes of their words, but rather clothe yourself in the living Word. Proverbs 30:5 says: *"Every word of God is flawless; he is a shield to those who take refuge in him" (NIV).*

If someone is constantly criticizing you and telling you that you are not good enough to achieve your goals, you should counter their words by telling yourself *"For I can do everything through Christ, who gives me strength" (Philippians 4:13-NLT).* Whenever you encounter verbal bullying, counter it with the Word of God. The enemy will say anything to discourage and keep you from experiencing the plan and power of God. Do not allow the devices of the enemy to prevent you from achieving your destiny.

Your response to being attacked with negative words should always be with prayer. This was exactly what Nehemiah and the people did when they were attacked. They prayed, *"Hear, O' our God, for we are despised; turn their reproach on their own heads, and give them as plunder to a land of captivity! Do not cover their iniquity, and do not let their sin be blotted out from before you; for they have provoked you to anger before the builders. So, we built the wall, and the entire wall was joined together up to half its height, for the people had a mind to work" (Nehemiah 4:4-6-NKJV).*

God was able to strengthen them and keep them focused on their goal. God tells us to *"Be anxious for nothing, but in everything by prayer and supplication with thanksgiving let your requests be made known to God" (Philippians 4:6-NKJV).* Prayer is the right response to any opposition. You may not be able to stop the enemy's mocking and critical words from reaching your ears, but you can stop the enemy's word from entering your heart.

The enemy's second attempt to discourage the people was by threats of force. *"Now it happened, when Sanballat, Tobiah, the Arabs, the Ammonites, and the Ashdodites heard that the walls of Jerusalem were being restored and the gaps were beginning to be closed, that they became very angry, and all of them conspired together to come and attack Jerusalem and create confusion. Nevertheless we made our prayer to our God, and because of them we set a watch against them day and night" (Nehemiah 4:7-9-NKJV).*

Again, Nehemiah and the people sought God's help through prayer. Not only did God strengthen them, He gave them wisdom to set a continuous watch so their enemies would not catch them off guard. God is your protector. He is a mighty deliverer and can assure your safety. Whenever you feel afraid of being harmed, remember the promise of Psalm 9:9-10: *"The LORD is a refuge for the oppressed, a stronghold in times of trouble, those who know your name trust in you, for you, LORD, have never forsaken those who seek you"* (NIV). Seek Him and you will find Him. Pray according to His will and He will hear you and give you help. Not only will He help you, but He will also give you His peace to protect your heart and mind.

Remember the enemy brings threats to intimidate you in order to discourage you. Deny discouragement and maintain your faith in God's word. Every time you feel threatened, confess out loud Psalm 124:8, *"Our [my] help is in the name of the LORD, the Maker of heaven and earth"* (NIV). Through prayer allow God to deal with your enemies. He will strengthen and settle your heart as you keep your mind set on the work at hand.

The enemy's third attempt to discourage the people was to promote compromise. *"Now it happened when Sanballat, Tobiah, Geshem the Arab, and the rest of our enemies heard that I had rebuilt the wall, and that there were no breaks left in it (though at that time I had not hung the doors in the gates), that Sanballat and Geshem sent to me, saying, "Come, let us meet together among the villages in the plain of Ono." But they thought to do me harm. So I sent messengers to them, saying, "I am doing a great work, so that I cannot come down. Why should the work cease while I leave it and go down to you?"* (Nehemiah 6:1-3-NKJV).

Now, the enemy is good for trying to get God's people to succumb to compromise. It is one of the quickest ways to cause the people of God to forfeit God's promises. We must be very careful not to fall into temptation by putting any confidence in the flesh. Never feel like you are strong enough to go on the enemy's territory and not be affected. Never give place to the enemy to cause you to fall from your own steadfastness. Do not fool yourself and think that the enemy wants to interact with you for your good. On the surface, it may appear harmless: "Let's get together and talk." No! Refuse to step into the enemy's traps. Whenever the enemy seeks you it is with one agenda: - to do you harm.

One of the greatest areas of compromise for God's people is sexuality. It is widely accepted in the culture for men and women to have casual sexual encounters, but it is inappropriate behavior for God's people. *"But among you there must not be even a hint of sexual immorality, or of any kind of impurity, or of greed, because these are improper for God's holy people" (Ephesians 5:3-NIV).* Do you not know that God is Holy and expects His children to be holy? The temptation to follow the trends of this world may be great, but God's grace to commit to sexual purity is greater. When you are committed to living a sexually pure life you are doing a great work, and you should not stop to compromise with the enemy. Remain encouraged and do not allow anything or anyone to take you away from the first work God has called you to: holy living. Remember, *"The temptations in your life are no different from what others experience. And God is faithful. He will not allow the temptation to be more than you can stand. When you are tempted, he will show you a way out so that you can endure" (1 Corinthians 10:13-NLT).* Continue the great work of obeying and honoring God.

The enemy's fourth attempt to discourage the people was to use scare tactics. *"Then Sanballat sent his servant to me as before, the fifth time, with an open letter in his hand. In it was written: It is reported among the nations, and Geshem says, that you and the Jews plan to rebel; therefore, according to these rumors, you are rebuilding the wall, that you may be their king. And you have also appointed prophets to proclaim concerning you at*

Jerusalem, saying, "There is a king in Judah!" Now these matters will be reported to the king. So come, therefore, and let us consult together. Then I sent to him, saying, "No such things as you say are being done, but you invent them in your own heart." For they all were trying to make us afraid, saying, "Their hands will be weakened in the work, and it will not be done." Now therefore, O' God, strengthen my hands. (Nehemiah 6:5-9-NKJV).

Nehemiah denounced the ridiculous charges of the enemy and refused to allow them to distract or deter him. As in previous attacks, he continued to pray. Nehemiah was a man of prayer. No matter how or when the enemy attacked him, he never stopped seeking God. Never allow the enemy's attacks to cause you to cease praying. Never give up on involving God in the matters of your life. In the secret place of prayer God will strengthen you and enable you to prevail over the enemy.

The end result of Nehemiah and the people's steadfastness was victory! Not only did God prosper them mightily by enabling them to accomplish all they set out to accomplish, but He also brought every plot of the enemy to nothing! God fought for His people and strengthened their hands. God is not partial, nor does He show favoritism. He will do the same for you when you make Him your defense. God was exalted and glorified through Nehemiah's trial. *"So the wall was finished on the twenty-fifth day of Elul, in fifty-two days. And it happened, when all our enemies heard of it, and all the nations around us saw these things, that they were very disheartened in their own eyes; for they perceived that this work was done by our God" (Nehemiah 6:15-16-NKJV).* When you deny discouragement you give God an opportunity to reveal His greatness in your life.

Nancy's Testimony:

It was my privilege to interview a good friend of mine with a powerful testimony of denying discouragement. Nancy Larson became a born-again Christian in 1973. She has served as an ordained minister and seasoned prayer warrior for over thirty years. Nancy speaks throughout the United States and has ministered on radio and television. She lives in Phoenix, Arizona with Tom, her husband of fifty-five years.

In 1985, just before the Thanksgiving holiday, Nancy discovered a lump in her breast. She went to see her doctor the following week. The doctor examined her and concluded that the lump was probably not cancerous, but advised her to go see a surgeon for a biopsy. As she left her doctor's office on her way to her car, the enemy spoke words of fear that she would not live to see her daughter get married or the birth of any of her grandchildren. Nancy quickly denied discouragement by rejecting the thoughts. A few days later the surgeon did the biopsy and it came back positive for cancer. She was instructed to go home, pack some clothes, and return to the hospital to have her mastectomy the following day. The surgeon told Nancy hers was an aggressive form of breast cancer that had already spread to nine lymph nodes. Only five to ten percent of women with this type of cancer survive. At that point Nancy felt that she had done something wrong for this to happen to her. The Holy Spirit immediately said to her, "That this is not from the hand of God, but from the hand of the enemy."

On the third night after having the mastectomy the enemy attempted to discourage Nancy again. As she lay in her hospital bed a terrible spirit of fear entered her room. Nancy was not fearful and she began to speak boldly to the presence saying, "You will be sorry you ever did this to me. I will be a stronger Christian than ever before. I will be closer to the Lord than ever before." Nancy was prepared for this encounter because a few days earlier the Lord had comforted Nancy's heart from the book of Isaiah. *"But now, thus says the LORD, who created you, O' Jacob, And He who formed you, O' Israel: Fear not, for I have redeemed you; I have called you by your name; you are Mine. When you pass through the waters, I will be with you; And through the rivers, they shall not overflow you. When you walk through the fire, you shall not be burned, nor shall the flame scorch you"* (Isaiah 43:1-2-NKJV). Nancy made a decision to believe the voice of the Lord and not the enemy. She knew the outcome of her trial would be a product of her choices, and she was determined to end up in the Lord's will.

Looking back, Nancy recalls thinking to herself that if she ever had cancer she would not tell anyone, but the Lord was making it clear that He wanted her to tell people about her cancer and the mastectomy. It hadn't occurred to her the Lord would use her experience as a ministry. All she knew was that she did not want to go through chemotherapy. She did not want to experience radiation after seeing how terribly it had affected her step-father's body. She wanted the Lord to heal her supernaturally so that she could avoid any type of cancer treatments. Nancy prayed fervently for her healing and one day the Lord spoke to her heart out of Ephesians 6:13. *"Wherefore take unto you the whole armor of God that ye may be able to withstand in the evil day, and having done all, to stand"* (Ephesians 6:13-KJV). The Lord told her that taking the chemotherapy was part of the "having done all." It was at that point that discouragement successfully entered into Nancy's heart. Accepting that it was part of God's plan for her to go through chemotherapy was very difficult to embrace. She began to question if she would ever be the same. Will she ever be able to do the things she once did? Yet, somehow, the Lord gave Nancy grace to go forward and begin treatment.

Between the second and third chemotherapy treatment Nancy had to once again deny discouragement. She caught her daughter's cold and got really sick. After her blood was drawn she was told that she did not have any white blood cells and had to be put into the hospital. While lying in her hospital bed in the middle of the night the spirit of death entered her room. She felt a dark, evil presence. She was physically at a low point and many times the enemy will come when you are at your weakest. As she lay in her hospital bed the spirit of death told her she was going to die. Although weak in her body, Nancy was strong in her spirit and took refuge in the Word of God. She knew that she would not die but would live to proclaim what the Lord has done *(Psalm 118:17-NIV)*. Nancy commanded the spirit to leave her and it did!

Through six months of chemotherapy Nancy's body continued to deteriorate and her spirit encountered many demonic attacks. She frequently felt too weak to leave the house, but would make it a point to attend church as often as she could. As she sat in church one Sunday night, concerned about losing her hair, the Lord spoke to her and said that it would only be for a time and her hair would grow back. The Lord assured her that He was with her and would take her through this trial. She felt that Jesus was standing right next to her and was convinced the cancer would not kill her. After completing all her treatments, it took about six weeks for Nancy to regain her strength and feel well again.

As a result of her experiences Nancy cautions people not to listen to anyone's horror stories or spend a lot of time researching their illnesses. Never put your focus on the disease, but keep what the Word says before you instead. Nancy believes a firm foundation is necessary to go through any trial and Jesus must be the foundation--not your church, spouse, family or friends. Make sure that the foundation is laid before the test comes.

Nancy continues to share her testimony in churches and women's events. She enjoys encouraging and praying for those who are physically and spiritually afflicted. Her message to them is to stay in the Word of God and stand on the scriptures. Do exactly what the Lord tells you to do, whether it is chemotherapy or something else. Nancy's trial was over within a year and she knew that the Lord had completely healed her. She has now been cancer-free for over twenty-eight years. The Lord took what the enemy had purposed for evil and turned it around for good. He has been using Nancy's testimony for His glory ever since.

The Lord is faithful to bring you through your afflictions victoriously. *"Many are the afflictions of the righteous, but the Lord delivers us from them all" (Psalm 34:19-NKJV).* The Lord is dependable. He will be with you no matter what you go through. I have learned through my trials and the trials of others that it is of vital importance that we hear from the Lord exactly how He wants to bring us through and to accept and obey His plan. If His plan is to heal through medicine or the laying on of hands, trust His wisdom. When we obey what the Lord tells us to do, we exercise our faith. Our faith is demonstrated in our obedience, not our plan. Your friend might have received a miracle healing, but, like Nancy, you may be led to take medicine. You are not faithless because your healing is not supernatural. Your faith is just as valid as anyone else when you obey the Lord's will. Remember, the key is in knowing His will and obeying it.

In every life the thief will come seeking an opportunity to bring destruction. The scriptures warn us that the thief comes to steal, kill and destroy *(John 10:10a)*. That is the enemy's only agenda. The good news is that Jesus comes to give life, and to give it in abundance! *(John 10:10b)*. We are presented with a choice. We can choose the enemy's destruction or the Lord's life. Choose life! When you find yourself in the midst of trouble, don't lose heart. Deny discouragement and receive the power Jesus offers you through faith in His Word.

5

WATCH YOUR WORDS

Do not use foul or abusive language. Let everything you say be good and helpful, so that your words will be an encouragement to those who hear them (Ephesians 4:29-NLT).

Training the tongue is incredibly difficult. Controlling what we say and do not say, is a discipline we must all develop. I love what is written in the third chapter of the book of James beginning at verse eight: *"But no man can tame the tongue. It is an unruly evil, full of deadly poison. With it we bless our God and Father, and with it we curse men, who have been made in the similitude of God. Out of the same mouth proceed blessing and cursing. My brethren, these things ought not to be so"* (NKJV). That is a piercing indictment on the use of our tongues.

The truth is, we have to be careful about all the words that we allow to come out of our mouths. It may seem innocent to speak in a derogatory manner or with light sarcasm, but every word we speak has power to create. We are made in the image and likeness of the Creator. He spoke words and created the entire visible and invisible worlds. That is incredible power! The scriptures reveal that *"the tongue can bring death or life and those who love to talk will reap the consequences"* (Proverbs 18:21-NLT). Thus, being thoughtful and strategic about the words we speak is not only right, but wise. Imagine how many problems we could avoid or eliminate if we did not allow negative words to come out of our mouths. Imagine how much stress we could prevent and peace we could enjoy simply by speaking words that edify.

Frustration often triggers reckless speaking. If it isn't yet obvious, you will soon come to the realization that *The Waiting Room* experience can be intensely frustrating. Knowing there are many opportunities to feel frustrated, be prepared for it and learn how to deal with it appropriately. There was a time when my picture should have appeared next to the definition of the word frustration. Frustration is the feeling of being upset or annoyed, especially due to inability to change or achieve something. I frequently felt this way before the creation of the Global Positioning System (GPS). If anybody is thankful for the GPS, it is me. I would get so upset when I could not find the address to the place I was going. It was easy for me to get turned around. I did not know anyone more directionally challenged than me, especially if I had to drive at night. I remember one day my frustration got the best of me. I was lost and so frustrated that I started to cry. Out of my frustration I began saying foolish things like, "I hate driving and I am never driving anywhere unfamiliar again," and, "I cannot drive anywhere without getting lost." What frustrated me most was feeling I should be able to follow simple directions, but I consistently failed to do so. Now, that might seem like a harmless example, but, believe me, the unconquered trigger of frustration has the potential to accelerate to far more damaging outcomes.

Imagine the frustration of a person looking for a job for many months receiving another rejection letter. In the midst of this type of frustration there is a temptation to speak negative words like, "I'll never find a job in this market," or, "My family and I will be thrown out in the streets," or, "God doesn't love me or answers my prayers." When these types of thoughts enter your mind you must quickly counter them with the life-giving words of God. *"Man shall not live by bread alone, but by every WORD that comes from the mouth of God" (Matthew 4:4-ESV).* Do not allow words that pronounce doom and demise to come out of your mouth. Do not pronounce anything negative about your life or future because what you are really doing is declaring a curse on yourself! Thinking it does not mean you have to speak it. It is easier to conquer the thoughts you keep contained in your mind than when your words give them life and they become strongholds.

Remember, your miracle begins in your mouth. Only allow the truth to proceed from your mouth. What is truth? God's Word is truth. Only say what God says about your life and future, and you will see your circumstances come in line with truth. It is critical that you know what God's Word teaches and that you apply His Word to every situation. The truth is empowering and it will help you avoid falling into error. When you find yourself in the midst of frustrating circumstances, instead of speaking carelessly, speak God's truth over those circumstances. For example, *"I know God is working in this for my good" (Romans 8:28).* Encourage yourself with the truth by boldly proclaiming, *"God will not withhold any good thing from me" (Psalm 84:11). "He will never leave me nor forsake me" (Hebrews 13:5). "My help comes from the Lord, who made heaven and earth" (Psalm 121:1). "I cast my cares on the LORD and He will sustain me; He will never let the righteous fall" (Psalm 55:22).* I could go on and on, but I am sure that you get my point.

Paula's Testimony:

My dear friend Paula went through a tremendous battle with her faith and her failure to watch her words made the battle even more difficult. After experiencing a number of disappointments over a period of years with leaders, church members, and Christian friends, Paula began to feel overwhelmingly unloved and resentful. It was not long until Paula decided to stop attending church altogether. I remember some of our conversations during that time being extremely awkward. Although I could discern how fragile and broken she had become, I also knew that her isolation was very dangerous. The enemy was very much involved in the process of her pulling away and wanted her far away from the oversight of spiritual leadership and fellowship of her brothers and sisters in Christ. The spiritual warfare was intense as I tried to help Paula recognize her errors. At times I felt like I was not only fighting against Satan's will to destroy Paula, but also her will to cooperate with his plans.

For a number of years I encouraged Paula to find a new church community and to continue confessing and hoping in the scriptures. Many times it seemed like my words were not registering. The more I attempted to encourage her, the more she seemed to resist and do the opposite of my advice. She had fallen into a broken and bitter place and, from my perspective, felt justified in lingering there. The longer she cleaved to resentment, the stronger her justification became to complain about and criticize church leaders, members, and even God. Her words became increasingly reckless each time we talked. I did whatever I could to help her see things differently, especially when I felt that she was charging God with evil. Her life was filled with many challenges, but God was not the blame. I did not think she could handle hearing that she was most likely her biggest problem. She would often say things like, "I am so sick of talking to Christians with perfect lives who are nothing more than judgmental." I took that as a signal for me to use extra precautions in sharing my views.

There were times when her venting would come off as nothing more than comical. We would both laugh as she jokingly described her lot in life. I remember one moment in particular when she said, "God made me a woman and gave me a womb just to torment me with a childless life." I had empathy for her on so many levels. I knew she was feeling pressure getting older and not being married. I also knew her desperate desire to have children. There were times her venting would go over the top. She would say, "I will never get married! My situation is hopeless! Every relationship has failed, and once again I am just another year older and still single." And, like a recorded message, I would pipe in and say, "Paula, you need to speak the truth, not your feelings." She talked as if God Himself was orchestrating her unhappiness, as if He took pleasure in her life consisting of working hard at a job she hated and ending the day husbandless and childless. I could not explain why it was taking so long for her to get married. I wished I could find her the perfect man. I prayed for her and with her for years, but relationship after relationship failed to progress into a promising future. Paula felt she hadn't anybody to live for. She desperately wanted someone to love and cherish, and for someone to love and cherish her. The only significant relationships in her life providing the love she craved in the form of family were her mother and her Husky, Corey.

Despite my heart being tender towards Paula, I still had to tell her the truth. The truth of what the scriptures say about how she should use her words. Scriptures like *Ephesians 4:29, "Do not use foul or abusive language. Let everything you say be good and helpful, so that your words will be an encouragement to those who hear them" (NLT). And Matthew 12:37, "for by your words you will be justified, and by your words you will be condemned" (ESV).* I tried to help her understand that even though she was terribly dissatisfied, she would still be held accountable to the Word of God. Unfortunately, when people are deeply wounded and deeply disappointed they tend to disregard the authority of the Word and rebel. Their actions challenge God that if He does not care about them, then they won't care about Him. This is not a wise position to take. God's ways are perfect and He deserves to be reverenced and honored despite our disappointments.

Once, Paula's reckless words severely crossed the line. I decided to call and check on her as I drove to the grocery store. In the past I had heard her slip-up and use profanity if she was very upset, but this day she was allowing profanity to roll out of her mouth without any restraint. I had never heard her so fired up. I knew she was under intense pressure at work and was dealing with some extremely difficult family issues, but I never expected that she would erupt under the weight. As I listened to her protest about how sick and tired she was of the circumstances of her life, I felt conflicted. My spirit was so grieved by the bold and brazen way she was talking and wanted to quickly shut her down, but my heart was concerned that she was much too fragile and would go over an emotional edge. Finally, I had to challenge her to see that her behavior was unacceptable and the profane manner in which she was talking was wrong. I tried my best to communicate that truth in a loving, Christ-like manner, but my attempts were not well received. Paula knew what the scriptures instructed, but she was not following the instructions. As her sister in the Lord, I felt obliged to love her by correcting her. She was going down a slippery path heading towards great destruction. *"He who guards his mouth and his tongue keeps himself from troubles"* states Proverb 21:23 *(AMP).* Paula's words had become lethal daggers in her hands, yet the person she was primarily hurting was herself. While I was pointing out that her conduct was unacceptable, Paula suddenly wanted to end the conversation. I am sure she wanted to call me a few choice words at that moment, but thank God our friendship meant enough to her to be worth preserving. After a few days we were able to calmly discuss what happened and move forward in our friendship.

A few months later, Paula experienced a breakthrough in the form of terrible tragedy and pain. Her twelve year old husky developed a life-threating tumor. After taking him to see a number of veterinarians, Paula learned that Corey's condition was very serious. Corey was the love and joy of Paula's life and his diagnosis was heartbreaking. I remember receiving text messages from her asking for prayer for his healing. She even asked if people would come to her house and lay hands on him and pray. Paula spared no effort or expense in his treatments. After experiencing compounding symptoms, Corey's pain became unbearable. It was difficult for him to eat, void or even sleep. I could not stand to hear his agonizing cries for the few minutes Paula and I spoke by phone, but poor Paula was enduring entire days and nights of it. Due to his complicated and confusing symptoms being misdiagnosed, Corey succumbed to his disease and died. I had been hoping and praying he would pull through for Paula's sake. I did not think she was ready to deal with such a loss, but deep inside I knew that, whenever it happened, it would be incredibly difficult for her to handle.

The day Corey died Paula sent out a sad and unexpected text message. She told a group of us that he had passed and she did not want anyone to call or text her for a month. She wanted to be left alone and would reach out to us when she was ready. I thought this would be the time she would want people to text and call. This should be the time to have people pray and lay on hands. However, I decided to respect Paula's wishes and not respond to her text message or try to call her.

Surprisingly, after only a few days, Paula reached out to me. I was not sure I was ready to have a conversation with her knowing it would be sad and gloomy. However, I felt compassion for her and wanted to be a good friend in her time of need. She began to share with me the difficult details of Corey's final days and what God had revealed to her. As she started to cry, she told me she had sensed that God wanted her to trust Him to heal her beloved pup, but she was wondering if she had lost sight of her faith in the process of trying to do all she could to save him. She questioned if she failed to trust God and relied too much on natural means. Through her tears she asked me if I thought her lack of faith caused her to lose him. I was not sure what to say or how to encourage her. I was purposely careful and inwardly prayerful that God would guide my words. I told her that I did not know the answer to that question, and some answers we may never receive on this side of heaven. I assured her that God knew that this would happen. We have to trust that God knows what He is doing. He gave her twelve wonderful years filled with Corey's love and she would always have those memories. Nothing can take the place that he has within her heart, but now she had an opportunity to love anew. Though one love had ended, God's love endures and never fails.

Somewhere between the indescribable pain and agony of living without her *canine boy,* as she had referred to him, God's truth was finally able to penetrate Paula's core. She could finally see the dark, ugly sin of her heart, her unforgiveness and self-righteous pride. God's light was able to lead her to repentance. It has been amazing to see how God used Paula's pain to help renew her faith and restore her focus on Him. He was no longer the distant and uncaring God she had portrayed Him to be with her words. She had been broken, but not destroyed; perplexed, but not in despair. She now recognized that God had been with her all along: through all the frustrations, disappointments, and hurts. Her bitterness did not run Him away, but her words prevented her from experiencing His grace. Paula has a new hunger for God's presence and a bold determination, now more than ever, to not allow Satan any room to work through her words.

My Testimony Trouble:

Reflecting on your story, how have you chosen to use your own words? If you are like me you probably have a few regrets. Many of us have let words slip out of our mouths that we either misspoke or should not have said at all. To this day, I regret the words of a testimony I shared at a good friend's party. Genesis (not her real name) wanted to bring friends, family and church members together to magnify the Lord through testimonies. We all gathered in her backyard and formed a great big circle. She began the process by sharing what the Lord had put on her heart.

Before we all went outside to the backyard, I shared with Genesis that a few weeks prior I experienced an unexpected hospital stay. I was on my way to take my youngest son, about six months old at the time, to his doctor's appointment. As I lifted his car seat to secure in place, I felt something snap in my groin area. Despite the slight discomfort I felt on my right side, I proceeded to buckle both kids into their car seats and drive to the appointment. By the time I reached the hospital the pain had intensified. I began to think that I should go to the emergency room, but decided to continue to my son's doctor's office. When we arrived at the check-in desk, the pain had become too great to ignore. I canceled the appointment and went directly to the emergency room. Within the hour I had called my husband to come and care for the kids, and I was rushed to emergency surgery for an ectopic pregnancy.

I had no idea I was pregnant and having another baby was nowhere on my agenda. Although I loved being at home raising my two children, I felt overwhelmed meeting their needs and the demands of my household. Coupled with the struggles I was having in my marriage, I could not imagine bringing another child into the equation. As I shared my testimony with the group, my casual response to my experience and my emphasis on being alright with the outcome was taken offensively.

Attempting to appear strong and victorious, I shared my experience without sensitivity to those longing for children or those having lost a child. I thought I was communicating that although my loss was a bad experience, the Lord worked in it for my good. I was encouraged. I was comforted. The Lord had made everything alright. Well, Genesis called me later and told me that a few people had commented that they had a problem with the things I shared. Thank God that my friend knew my heart and explained to them that I did not say what I said correctly. After thinking about how I shared my experience, I understood why some people took offense. I was embarrassed and sorry for my insensitivity and wished that I could go back and do it over.

Unfortunately, the words we say cannot be retracted. It is impossible to get them back once we let them come out of our mouths. I am certain that a man named Jephthah wished it was possible to erase the words he spoke when he made a very foolish vow. Judges, Chapter 11, describes his foolish vow and the unimaginable price he had to pay for his words.

Jephthah's Vow:

Jephthah was the son of Gilead. Gilead fathered him with a prostitute. He also fathered other sons with his wife. After these sons grew up they demanded that Jephthah depart from them since he was the son of another woman. They refused to allow him to inherit anything in their father's house. So, Jephthah fled to another land. Years later the elders of Gilead asked him to return to help them fight their enemy the Ammonites. After some convincing, Jephthah agreed, but his desire to conquer their enemy led to him making a foolish vow. *"And Jephthah made a vow to the LORD, and said, "If you will give the Ammonites into my hand, then whatever* comes out of the doors of my house to meet me, when I return in peace from the Ammonites, shall be the LORD's, and I will offer it up for a burnt offering" (Judges 11:30-31-ESV). Jephthah was victorious and he and his people greatly defeated the Ammonites.

Now, when Jephthah returned home his only child came running out of the house to meet him with timbrels and dancing. Jephthah's celebration quickly turned into lamentation. In anguish, he tells his daughter that she had brought him low and caused him great trouble. He had made a vow to the Lord and could not recant. Truly, it was not his daughter who caused him the great trouble, but the words that he spoke out of his mouth. Whoever guards his mouth and tongue, keeps his soul from troubles (Proverbs 21:23-AMP). Jephthah should never have made such a foolish vow in the first place. In my opinion, he should have been specific and vowed to offer up a bull, lamb, or goat, not a 'whatever'. Sadly, after allowing his daughter to spend two months mourning her lost future with her friends, Jephthah fulfilled his vow.

This may be an extreme example of the consequences of speaking foolish words, but the reality is our words have the power to cause great devastation. Remember: death and life are in the power of your tongue. You must use your tongue wisely and only speak words that will bring good and life to you and others. Avoid being presumptuous and insensitive. Do not let frustration get the best of you. Bring all your emotions to the Lord in prayer and ask Him to give you grace to overcome the temptation to speak inappropriately. Remember, your miracle begins in your mouth.

6

GUARD YOUR HEART

Above all else, guard your heart, for everything you do flows from it (Proverbs 4:23-NIV).

For the first twelve years of my life, I was raised by my mother in a single-parent household. I am the second eldest of five siblings. My family was poor and struggled financially until my mother met and married my step-father. Economically things began to improve, but spiritually we remained deprived. In our household faith was never a pursuit or priority. Typical of many spiritually inactive families, I was told we had a religious affiliation. That affiliation was Catholicism, although during my upbringing we never practiced the faith. I did not know anything about the Bible, Church or God. The only thing I knew about praying was saying 'Jesus wept' before I ate and 'Now I lay me down to sleep' at bedtime.

One Sunday, a friend of the family took me and my eldest brother to church with her. I believe this experience initially aroused my interest in knowing God. I still remember my first God-thoughts. I was about eight years old. We lived in a high-rise building on the south side of Chicago. As I looked out the window of our eighth floor apartment I began to wonder about Heaven and if God was watching me. I wanted Him to talk to me and answer some questions. One night, I took my fingernail and wrote a question on my leg (I do not recall the question) and hoped that in the morning God would have written an answer. Of course, when I woke up all I saw was my question etched in my dry skin. My desire to discover God began to grow from that point on, but took many years to be fully experienced.

After I graduated from high school I joined the United States Navy. While stationed in Yokosuka, Japan I had my first encounter with God. A coworker invited me and another friend to attend her church service. I do not think either one of us knew that she would be preaching, or even that she was a preacher. All I knew was that she spoke with a passion and conviction that was foreign, yet refreshing to my ears. Her words impacted our hearts and souls. The words she shared resonated so deeply with both of us that all we could do was hold one another and cry. I did not understand what I was feeling then, but later I understood that we had been in the presence of the Living God. This was especially amazing to me because I never knew that God was a Living God. I never knew that He was personal and desired to interact with me.

From that point on, my eyes were opened and I began to see God working in the lives of people all around me. It seemed that every month someone in my barracks surrendered their life to Jesus Christ. One person after another would share with me how their lives had been changed by the Lord. They stopped drinking alcohol, using profanity, and going to the dance club. Each expressed how the truth of the Bible had influenced the changes in their lives. The more I was exposed to their faith, the greater the battle raged inside of me. I was not ready to make a commitment to the Bible's way of living, but I knew I was terminally unhappy. I could not deny the emptiness, bitterness, and brokenness I carried inside.

A few years after being honorably discharged from the Navy, I surrendered my life to Jesus Christ. It was the best decision I had ever made. My only regret is that I wish I would have made the decision sooner. It happened after one of my coworkers invited me to attend his church service. The church was quite a distance from my house. It only had a handful of members, but the people seemed to share a genuine bond. I was drawn to the family atmosphere and impressed by the demonstrations of love the members expressed. I visited a second time and at the end of the service I found myself standing before the Pastor asking to join the church. I had not previously given any thought to joining; it seemed to involuntarily happen before I knew what I was saying.

That afternoon, when I went home to my apartment, I had an extraordinary encounter with the Living God. As I entered my bedroom, the presence of God was there. I found myself on my knees in the middle of the room crying from the depths of my soul. I felt sorry and convicted for how I had been living. In that moment I was fully aware of my sinfulness and the pain it had caused the Holy God. All I could do was cry and ask God to forgive me for all of my sins. I'm not certain how long I was on my knees repenting, but I remember how renewed I felt when it was all over. I knew that I was born-again that day. I could not explain how, I certainly did not know all the terminology or theology, but I knew I was not the same. Immediately, as soon as I stood up, I could sense the leading of the Holy Spirit. It was incredible to me (and still is). I had a supernatural knowing I could not explain. I knew there were things needing to be removed from my life, and new things had to be added. I knew to throw away certain types of clothes, pictures, and music. I knew to break up with my boyfriend, stop having sex, cursing, etc. My old life was passing away and the new life had begun *(2 Corinthians 5:17)*!

That same day the Holy Spirit began the process of transforming and sanctifying my life. The first lessons He taught me remain the foundations of my faith. He told me to start, right away, reading through the entire Bible and developing a daily prayer discipline. Then, He revealed to me the key to maturing and maintaining soundness in the faith. His words have stuck with me all these years and continue to be the fundamental focus of my spiritual life. The key is to know and protect the condition of your heart and the state of your mind.

It is important to be aware of the health of your heart and mind. You are the best evaluator and assessor of the condition of your heart and the state of your mind. You have an up-close view of the intimate thoughts of your mind and desires within your heart. It is not to your advantage to ignore or deny an unhealthy state or condition of either. You must quickly detect a wrong state or condition and correct it. Refusing or neglecting to acknowledge and address the need for change can allow issues to become deeply rooted and give the enemy a foothold to work. As God's children we are called to walk in truth. We must accept and gladly receive the truth even when it conflicts with our thoughts and desires. We must apply the truth to our hearts and minds in order to access its power.

It is also important to *protect* the health of your heart and mind. Once the process of renewal and cleansing has been experienced, you must commit to maintaining your restoration. It would be highly disappointing to complete the hard work involved in restoration just to repeat the process. You do not want to redo any work. There is too much at stake. Your restoration fosters freedom, and your freedom is much too valuable to be treated lightly. Your mind and heart are protected as you continue to walk in the truth that secured your restoration. *"So if the Son sets you free; you will be free indeed" (John 8:36-NIV).* The Lord has purchased your liberty with the greatest price: His life. The blood of Jesus was shed so you can be totally restored to the creation God initially intended for you. You do not have to live as a wounded soul. There is help and healing through Jesus Christ for everyone who believes.

During these early lessons the Holy Spirit revealed that my mind has a constant need of renewing, and my heart is in constant need of cleansing. Renewal and cleansing are accomplished only by the truth of God's Word. The Word is living and powerful and has the ability to correct thinking and heal damaged emotions. As the mind is renewed it becomes sound and healthy. As the heart is cleansed it becomes pure and clean. I find myself often praying the words of *Psalm 51:10 (KJV): "Create in me a clean heart O' God and renew a right spirit within me."* It is essential to pursue a sound mind and a pure heart because your decisions and desires are a direct product of their state and condition. When the mind is corrupt, your decisions will reek of corruption. When the heart is unclean, your desires will be defiled. We must seek after the righteousness of the Word to experience the healing required to live victoriously. Frequently assess the health of your mind and heart by evaluating your thoughts and desires. God instructs us to guard our hearts diligently because everything we do flows from our hearts. *"Above all else, guard your heart, for everything you do flows from it" (Proverbs 4:23-NIV).*

Satan Seeks A Heart:

In the Gospel of Matthew the disciples asked Jesus to explain a parable that He taught the people. In chapter fifteen Matthew writes: *"Then Peter answered and said to Him, "Explain this parable to us." So Jesus said, "Are you also still without understanding? Do you not yet understand that whatever enters the mouth goes into the stomach and is eliminated? But those things which proceed out of the mouth come from the heart, and they defile a man. For out of the heart proceed evil thoughts, murders, adulteries, fornications, thefts, false witness, blasphemies: These are the things which defile a man, but to eat with unwashed hands does not defile a man" (15-20-NKJV).*

Jesus reveals some intriguing truths through his explanation of the parable. He masterfully exposes the root of the problem. First, what comes out of your mouth has a direct correlation to what is in your heart. Second, when you allow sin to enter your heart it will defile you. To be defiled means to be corrupted, tarnished, polluted, dishonored, degraded or ruined. These strong words depict a sobering reality of the toxic effect of sin in one's life. At the core of all evil is the sin that enters the heart. When sin enters your heart it poisons your whole being. This further proves how imperative it is to guard your heart and keep it free of sin. Guarding the heart must be a top priority. You cannot take it lightly or be ignorant of the responsibility. Everything is at stake because the products of an unhealthy heart will have a devastating impact on your relationships, career, ministry, and legacy.

The enemy is fully aware of the process and knows where to target his stealthy attacks. Sadly, many people are oblivious to the reality of spiritual warfare and that Satan is constantly seeking an opportunity to bring destruction. Life is one big combat zone, and the heart of man is the intended target. You must be knowledgeable of Satan's strategies used in his attacks. For example, the Apostle Paul wrote to the church in Corinth concerning a sensitive issue related to the heart. A man in the church committed a serious offense and the church leadership disciplined him. After exercising sufficient punishment, Paul encouraged the church to forgive and comfort the man so excessive sorrow would not overwhelm him. Paul wanted to ensure the hearts of those in leadership were right toward this person, so Satan would not gain advantage through the hardness of their hearts. In other words, these men had to guard and protect their hearts from being defiled by unforgiveness. If they were unable to forgive and demonstrate love to the man who committed the offense, their unforgiveness would leave their hearts unprotected. Guarding your heart not only requires watching what you allow in, but also what you allow to come out.

Satan's works can thrive in an unguarded heart. What begins as an offense can progress into bitterness, hatred, and even murder. Remember Judas Iscariot, son of Simon? He was one of the original twelve disciples, but would become Jesus' betrayer. He betrayed Jesus for thirty pieces of silver and later regretted what he had done and hung himself *(Matthew 26:15; 27:3-5)*. How is it possible for a person to have intimate access and fellowship with Jesus Christ, God in the flesh, and then betray him to be put to death? How could Judas witness countless demonstrations of God's power through healing, performing miracles, casting out demons, and raising the dead, yet not believe in Christ? My theory is that Judas' heart was poisoned by the sin of pride. This sin left unattended eventually defiled him.

Judas must have possessed strong management and leadership skills. He was the treasurer and overseer of all the economic affairs in Jesus' ministry. He distributed money to help the poor, made purchases for the needs of the ministry, and most likely received any monetary donations to the work. His was a trusted and powerful position. At some point during his stewardship Judas became dissatisfied. He expressed displeasure with how Mary chose to use her precious perfume. To Mary it was worship, but Judas saw it as a financial decision. Why was this potential profit wasted on the Master's feet when it could have been sold for a lot of money to help the poor? Judas did not actually care about helping the poor, but was more interested in helping himself. *"Then Mary took about a pint of pure nard, an expensive perfume; she poured it on Jesus' feet and wiped his feet with her hair. And the house was filled with the fragrance of the perfume. But one of his disciples, Judas Iscariot, who was later to betray him, objected, "Why wasn't this perfume sold and the money given to the poor? It was worth a year's wages." He did not say this because he cared about the poor but because he was a thief; as keeper of*

the money bag, he used to help himself to what was put into it"
(John 12:3-6 NIV).

Judas, full of pride, considered his opinion superior and his work worth whatever he chose to take for himself. I would even venture to speculate that his pride clouded his judgment to the point he thought he was a better administrator and leader than Jesus. By his actions we see he determined in his mind that Jesus was unfit to lead and should be removed as Master. How else could he agree to betray an innocent man? Judas' heart had become completely open to evil, and Satan, who goes about looking for an opportunity to establish his evil agenda, jumps at the chance to enter him. The outcome will never be positive when we allow Satan to operate through us. Just as Judas' life was utterly destroyed, so goes everyone who dares to live with an unguarded heart for Satan to work through.

Here is the good news: Jesus has given us a great Helper, the Holy Spirit. The Holy Spirit empowers believers to live a life of faithfulness to God. We have not been left in the war zone of life to make it on our own. The Father sent His greatest gift: Jesus. Jesus sent His greatest gift: the Holy Spirit. The Holy Spirit is revealed in scripture as the third divine person of the Godhead. He fulfills many functions in the life of a believer. He teaches, counsels, comforts, intercedes, leads, convicts, equips, strengthens, cleanses, sanctifies, liberates and much more. As we submit our lives to His leadership, He will help us protect our hearts from the destructive nature of sin. The Lord knew as long as we are in the flesh we would have a proclivity to weakness. However, the Holy Spirit helps us in all of our weaknesses. We were called to be free from the enslavement of sin! *"Stand fast therefore in the liberty in which Christ has made you free and do not be entangled again with a yoke of bondage" (Galatians 5:1-KJV).*

The Word of the Lord is true. If we live by the Spirit we will not fulfill the desires of our flesh *(Galatians 5:16)*. The desires of the Spirit and the desires of the flesh are contrary. When tempted by evil, ask the Holy Spirit to help in resisting and to strengthen so evil passion and desire may be put to death. The man who endures temptation is blessed and shall receive the crown of life. I believe that means that when we reach a level of maturity to consistently deny temptation, we will gain the Lord's power and authority over that sin. There is never any excuse to succumb to sin. We cannot blame people, God, or Satan. God never tempts anyone with evil. Satan encourages disobedience (remember Eve in the garden?), but it is our own lust and desires that draw us away to be tempted. When lust is conceived, it brings forth sin and when sin is complete it brings forth death *(James 1:15)*. No one is exempt; facing temptation is a common part of life for everyone, but even in temptation God is faithful. He will not allow us to be tempted beyond our ability to handle it and will give us wisdom to avoid falling into sin's trap *(1 Corinthians 10:13)*. It is not sin to be tempted, Jesus himself was tempted but did not sin *(Matthew 4:1-10)*. Jesus resisted temptation and is also able to help us to resist it. *"So then, since we have a great High Priest who has entered heaven, Jesus the Son of God, let us hold firmly to what we believe. This High Priest of ours understands our weaknesses, for he faced all of the same testings we do, yet he did not sin. So let us come boldly to the throne of our gracious God. There we will receive his mercy, and we will find grace to help us when we need it most"* *(Hebrews 4:14-16-NLT)*.

When we are in Christ, the passions and desires of our flesh have been crucified with Him. Do not allow them to be resurrected. Fight against every passion and desire that is of the flesh. *"Now the works of the flesh are manifest, which are these; adultery, fornication, uncleanness, lasciviousness, Idolatry, witchcraft, hatred, variance, emulations, wrath, strife, seditions, heresies, envying, murders, drunkenness, revellings, and such like: of the which I tell you before, as I have also told you in time past, that they which do such things shall not inherit the kingdom of God"* (Galatians 5:19-21-KJV). Do not entertain the ideas or thoughts of evil. Do not practice evil works. The Holy Spirit will convict your hearts when you begin to go astray. Respond to His conviction by repenting immediately. Then, allow Him to transform you into the likeness of Jesus Christ.

While you work diligently to keep destructive things out of your heart, you must also work diligently to allow the Holy Spirit to place productive things into your heart. Our character comes from within, and Christ-like character is specifically developed by the Holy Spirit. The evidence of His work in your life is demonstrated when you possess love, joy, peace, patience, kindness, goodness, faithfulness, gentleness and self-control *(Galatians 5:23)*. These nine characteristics are called the *fruit of the Spirit* and are essential for maturity and victory in faith. It is important to allow the Holy Spirit to cultivate these characteristics in our hearts. They provide the needed protection for guarding our hearts, and we will discover the many benefits of possessing these characteristics as we continue to grow in the Lord and live by faith.

As you endeavor to do God's will and experience all His promises, I encourage you to make the Holy Spirit your best friend. The Holy Spirit is a distinct person with a personality. He has knowledge, intellect, emotions and his own will to make decisions that coincide with the Father's desires. He is described as a gentle dove who can be grieved, and can be trusted with all of your heart. Your heart is completely safe with Him and you can be completely honest and transparent in His presence. Like a best friend, He will be a tremendous support throughout all the seasons of life. He will remain loyal through good and difficult times. He is always ready and available to minister to your needs and help you obtain victory in the faith. A relationship with the Holy Spirit is special and irreplaceable. Never forget He is right there with you in *The Waiting Room.* Listen for His voice guiding you through the waiting process and bringing you closer to entering your opened door.

DON'T LIMIT YOURSELF

For I know the plans I have for you, declares the Lord. Plans to prosper you and not harm you, plans to give you hope and a future (Jeremiah 29:11-NIV).

Every time I stop to think about what Jeremiah 29:11 is actually saying, I get excited. That God has an awesome plan for me is beyond thrilling. God has an awesome plan for the lives of every one of His children. His plan is designed to make your life increasingly better. You may wonder why God doesn't give all the good He has planned at once. Why must we wait to receive a good future? As a parent, you would never give your child every benefit and blessing at once. You would use wisdom and wait until you knew that your child was mature enough to be appreciative and responsible. It may be your plan to give your child an expensive, rare painting you inherited from your parents. Knowing the intentions of your good plan will bring excitement and encouragement to your child; you will still be wise and wait until the right time before executing your plan.

God's plan is designed to bring encouragement today and give many good things to look forward to tomorrow. From the very beginning of your life, God has planned for you to flourish. You were created to prosper! God desires and delights in your fruitfulness so much that He has given you a life without limits. Living by faith is a limitless life. This is not, however, to be confused with a life without boundaries. Boundaries are wise and for your safety and well-being. Boundaries like do not worry, but pray instead. Do not steal, but work with your hands. Do not commit adultery, but remain faithful to your own spouse. These are all wise boundaries. When you respect and follow all the boundaries God has instructed through His Word, you will experience the protection and security it provides.

If you desire to experience God's plans you must live by faith. Living by faith is living without natural limits. To live by faith is to live a life of great possibilities; a life of great hope. *"If you can believe, all things are possible to him who believes" (Mark 9:23-NKJV).* Your only limits will be the ones you set by your thinking. Remember: God sets your boundaries, but you are the one setting limits. Your inability to believe God's Word will bring limits to your life every time. The disciples asked Jesus to explain why they experienced limitations in their effort to achieve deliverance for a young boy. Jesus told them their lack of faith was the cause.

"Lord, have mercy on my son, for he is an epileptic and suffers severely; for he often falls into the fire and often into the water. So I brought him to your disciples, but they could not cure him." Then Jesus answered and said, "O' faithless and perverse generation, how long shall I bear with you? Bring him here to Me." And Jesus rebuked the demon and it came out of him; and the child was cured that very hour. Then the disciples came to Jesus privately and said, "Why could we not cast it out?" So Jesus said to them, "Because of your unbelief; for assuredly I say to you, if you have faith as a mustard seed, you will say to this mountain, "Move from here to there," and it will move; and nothing will be impossible for you (Matthew 17:15-20-NKJV).

Unfortunately, we can be just like the disciples: failing to successfully exercise the authority given to us by Jesus Christ due to our lack of faith. Jesus gave His disciples power and authority to cast out demons, the very thing they were asked to do, but, because they lacked faith, the hand of the evil one was not moved.

Before Jesus liberated us we were captives and prisoners of the evil one. When Jesus set us free He opened the prison doors. Unbelief would be to remain in the cell and under the dictates of the evil one. A faithless and perverse generation refuses to respond to God's divine power and authority. Faith comes by hearing the Word of God and believing it. Faith is the gateway to experiencing God's divine power. If you have faith as a mustard seed, then *you can undo what the evil one has done*. You can say to the mountain: move from here to there. You can command the obstacles the enemy has planted to hinder you *to move!* You can command the corrupt seeds that the enemy has planted *to be uprooted!* You can lay hands on the afflicted and command the demons *to come out* and not to enter again! Hallelujah!

We never have to accept the works of the evil one. We should never agree with anything the evil one does. Do not allow the enemy to limit your life in any way. Has the evil one attacked your body with infirmity? Don't accept it! Speak the Word of life over yourself and undo what the evil one has done. Has the evil one attacked your character? Don't accept it! Speak the Word of life over yourself and undo what the evil one has done. Has the evil one attacked your marriage? Don't accept it! Together, speak the Word of life over your union and undo what the evil one has done. When you discern the evil one attacking your children, resources, relationships or opportunities: take authority and speak the Word of life over that situation, declaring "No weapon formed against me shall prosper and every tongue that rises up against me in judgment is condemned." For example, I begin by identifying the weapon and calling it by name. If fear is what I feel is against me, I would say: "Fear, you will not prosper against me. I cast down and condemn the lie that you will hurt or harm me. By the power and authority of Jesus Christ given to me I cast down every lying imagination and stronghold in my mind that has exalted itself over the truth of God's Word. I take dominion over all my thoughts insist my thinking be just as Christ has instructed in the name of Jesus!"

The good news of the Gospel is summed up in this: *the works of evil one are not final.* We must be able to discern the works of darkness. Anything that is not working according to God's awesome plan for your life involves the enemy. I guarantee the evil one is working against you in that area. God is, and will always be, *for* us. Failure is not part of His good plan for us. His desire is that we succeed and not fail. He doesn't want us to just have meager success. He wants us to have increasing and sustained success. Believe in that truth and don't allow anything to convince you otherwise. Make up in your mind that you will not limit yourself through unbelief! Whatever you are asking for in God's will you can receive. Whatever you are seeking in God's will you can find. Whatever door you are knocking on in God's will can be opened.

Have you been asking for financial increase and feel you are stuck with poor income-generating options? You may have some challenges to overcome, but don't allow erroneous thinking to limit your faith. First, make sure you are faithful in the stewardship of the little you have, and then God will increase your portion and promote you to greater stewardship. It is possible for you to increase, if you can only believe.

Are you seeking a spouse, but feel anxious because the flower of your youthfulness is fading? Don't allow age to limit your good future. God's good plans for us do not expire. God says marriage is an honorable experience and He who finds a wife finds a good thing and obtains favor from the Lord *(Proverbs 18:22).* Are you prepared to be found, my sister? Are you prepared to lead and love a wife, my brother? When you can answer yes to the question that applies to you, then nothing but you can hinder your success. Do not let the delay discourage you. Do not allow the delay to cause you to cast aside your hope, for God is faithful and can be trusted to keep His promises.

Heather's Testimony:

A dear friend of mine has an amazing testimony of overcoming intimidation. Her story reveals how she chose not to limit herself in *The Waiting Room* of an extraordinary promotion. Our friendship is the product of a divine connection. From the first time we met everything about our lives just clicked. Our lives complement one another and we became best of friends, seemingly overnight. There have been few people in my life where I sensed God divinely brought us together, and Heather (not her real name) is definitely one of those people.

Heather was a vice president in the Law Department of a Fortune 100 Company. She managed a diverse team of over forty legal and business professionals located in nine domestic and overseas offices. Heather was also a member of the General Counsel's Executive Leadership Team with responsibility for the global coordination of key strategic partnerships, guidance on governance issues, standardized processes, and broader customer communication. She ensured that all facets of key customer relationships were aligned with the overall organizational strategy.

After thirteen years with the company, Heather was tasked a unique high profile project to manage for the office of the CEO. As a result, Heather became a target of a senior leader's jealousy. His blatant disrespect not only made working on the project unpleasant, it started to corrode her desire to remain with the company. Heather had reached her potential in her role, many of her colleagues were leaving, and the company's performance metrics were dismal. These circumstances, combined with working with this difficult team member, sent Heather deeper into her prayer closet.

Throughout the project, Heather fasted and prayed for wisdom and grace. God was faithful to help her maintain her professionalism and continue to perform her job well, despite the frustration and challenges. During this difficult season, professionally, there were also changes for her, personally. Her nanny resigned and the Christian school her children attended notified her they would be closing their doors the following year. Initially these changes were upsetting, but Heather soon realized God was closing these doors to prepare for the great door He would soon open. God began to direct Heather's steps through her *Waiting Room* and renew her strength as she relied on Him.

The door He led her to was unexpected. Over the years Heather had developed many strong external client-customer relationships. One customer in particular wanted her to work for him. He felt she was such a dynamic leader with demonstrated professional success, that she would be a great addition to his company and senior executive leadership team. Although honored by the offer, Heather rejected the consideration due to a potential conflict of interest-- the two companies were in negotiations on a deal. Heather went a step further to maintain her integrity by informing her boss about the offer. Her boss, sensing the company was at risk of losing one of its top performers, offered Heather a raise and an impressive retention bonus to continue working for the company. The promotion and bonus helped to recognize Heather as a valued team member but, although she appreciated the increase in salary, her heart was slipping further away from the company. The negotiations successfully ended and Heather found herself once again faced with an unexpected opened door. The same customer presented her with a final once-in-a-lifetime offer. Heather had desired a new challenge and had been praying for a new professional opportunity, but this offer was exceedingly, abundantly above anything she had ever imagined. The position was grander in scope than any previous role and the financial offer matched that of a far more experienced professional. The expectations of her overseeing all legal transactions, ensuring overall legal compliance, working with a company board, and preparing a company to go from private to public caused Heather to question her capabilities, but, because she knew that Almighty God was her help, she refused to limit herself by leaning on her own understanding *(Proverbs 3:5)*.

Heather's boss was not happy with her decision to leave the company, but reluctantly gave his blessing. Trusting God and being obedient to His voice made this one of the best decisions of Heather's life. She joined her new company as General Counsel earning twice what she previously earned. By her second year her salary increased more than $100,000 with bonuses which added up into the millions. Today she is the Chief Administrative Officer and an official multi-millionaire.

Heather no longer struggles with intimidation and readily shares how God gave her exceeding wisdom and grace to achieve the desire of her heart. God taught her that she will never have to earn her portion and no one can take it away. Heather uses her testimony to show others what God can do when you trust Him. She loves to encourage others to seek to glorify God in their lives rather than striving for material blessings. Heather has learned from her experience that, when your motivation is to glorify God, He will exceed your expectations.

You may feel intimidated by the expectations which accompany your goals or desires. You may feel intimidated by insufficiencies you feel you have. The truth is: neither expectations nor insufficiencies, no matter how real or unreal, can hinder you from receiving what God has already planned to give you. Move forward and trust Him beyond your feelings of intimidation. God is not partial. God created you to prosper. Your future is good no matter what God has planned. Trust God with all your heart and seek Him for guidance to experience your desires. Consider if Heather had not trusted God by acting beyond her feelings of intimidation, she may never have experienced the blessings she is currently enjoying. Do not lose heart! Remember, your faith is in God's power not your own. He knows the plans He has for you. Plans to prosper you and not harm you, plans to give you a hope and a future *(Jeremiah 29:11)*. *Prepare your faith to prosper and God will establish your good future.*

King Joash's Story:

Do not to limit yourself by allowing your attitude to become toxic in *The Waiting Room*. The way you think and feel will be reflected in your conduct. Your attitude can be an expression of favor or disfavor. Problems arise when feelings of disfavor are demonstrated inappropriately in behavior. Maintain a positive attitude even when you lack motivation. A poor attitude has no benefit and the outcome can produce lifelong regrets.

Joash, King of Israel, was facing the threat of war and exacerbated his problems with his poor attitude. The Syrian army was preparing to invade the Israelite kingdom. King Joash was not only distraught about the invasion, but troubled because the prophet Elisha was dying. He had relied on Elisha to proclaim God's purpose and plan. Elisha was the mouthpiece of God and his voice was about to be silenced permanently. King Joash was faced with his desperate need for God's guidance while losing his confident guide. He rushed to Elisha for instructions to defeat the Syrian army and secure victory for Israel. In his feeble and near-death state Elisha proclaimed the Lord's victory and what King Joash must do:

Elisha had become sick with the illness of which he would die. Then Joash the king of Israel came down to him, and wept over his face, and said, "O' my father, my father, the chariots of Israel and their horsemen!" And Elisha said to him, "Take a bow and some arrows." So he took himself a bow and some arrows. Then he said to the king of Israel, "Put your hand on the bow." So he put his hand on it, and Elisha put his hands on the king's hands. And he said, "Open the east window"; and he opened it. Then Elisha said, "Shoot"; and he shot. And he said, "The arrow of the LORD's deliverance and the arrow of deliverance from Syria; for you must strike the Syrians at Aphek till you have destroyed them." Then he said, "Take the arrows"; so he took them. And he said to the king of Israel, "Strike the ground"; so he struck three times, and stopped. And the man of God was angry with him, and said, "You should have struck five or six times; then you would have struck Syria till you had destroyed it! But now you will strike Syria only three times" (2 Kings 13:14-19- NKJV).

Although King Joash followed the Prophet Elisha's instructions, he did it with a toxic attitude. The arrows he was shooting were proclaimed as symbolic of the Lord's deliverance. He was supposed to approach the exercise with a militant, combat-like intensity as a true warrior should. Yet, his halfhearted compliance cost the Israelites total victory over their enemy. It was not the Lord's intention for Israel to strike Syria three times, but until they were completely destroyed.

Obeying the Lord's voice with the proper attitude is necessary to experience the Lord's promise as He intends. We must not allow a toxic attitude to limit us and cause us to fall short of the Lord's intended blessings.

8

REMAIN PRAYERFUL

Always be joyful. Always keep on praying. No matter what happens, always be thankful, for this is God's will for you who belong to Christ Jesus (1 Thessalonians 5:16 -18 TLB).

I once heard a pastor say: *when you inhale a worry, you should exhale a prayer.* Prayer is as essential to sustaining spiritual life as oxygen is to sustaining physical life. Prayer is the divinely appointed means through which we can commune with the Living God and establish His plan and purpose for our life. God is the One who ordains and orders prayer. **Prayer is an act of faith and obedience.** *"Let us therefore come boldly to the throne of grace, that we may obtain mercy and find grace to help in time of need" (Hebrews 4:16-NKJV).* I consider it a privilege and an honor to approach the throne of God. Being granted the opportunity to bring a request before the True and Living God is an extraordinary gift. To come into the presence of the Eternal God, Creator of all things and receive wisdom, mercy, peace, strength, healing and help is invaluable.

Prayer must be a priority. Daily set aside a time to pray, and view this time not as a duty but as a privilege. The effectual, fervent prayer of a righteous man is powerful. Keep a prayer journal and write specific prayer requests for yourself and others. Also, record the answers you receive to your prayers. Keep in mind that prayer is a two-way communication. You talk and God listens. God talks and you listen. Oftentimes it is easy for us to talk to God, but difficult for us to hear His voice. Learning to clearly distinguish God's voice is crucial. We can mistake His voice for our own thoughts or the voice of the Enemy. Satan can speak to us and is rightly referred to as the great deceiver *(John 8:44)*.

Thankfully, God has provided some sure ways for us to know whether we are truly hearing His voice. There are several ways we can test what we hear to make sure it is God speaking:

1. Consistency with the Word of God - *All Scripture is given by inspiration of God, and is profitable for doctrine, for reproof, for correction, for instruction in righteousness, that the man of God may be complete, thoroughly equipped for every good work (2 Timothy 3:16-17-NKJV).* Be sure what you're hearing is consistent with the truth of God's Word. God will never contradict His Word. He will never instruct you to disobey His Word or affirm you in sin.

2. Witness of the Holy Spirit - *For those who are led by the Spirit of God are the children of God (Romans 8:14-NIV).* The Holy Spirit's guidance will always be consistent with God's Word. He will often confirm what God has revealed to you.

3. Voice of the Prophetic - *Do not smother the Holy Spirit. Do not scoff at those who prophesy, but test everything that is said to be sure it is true, and if it is, then accept it (1 Thessalonians 5:19-21-TMB).* God continues to use His prophets to reveal His heart and mind. Test each prophesy by the scriptures and insight provided by the Holy Spirit before you accept it.

4. Wisdom of Godly Counsel - *Where no counsel is, the people fall: but in the multitude of counsellors there is safety (Proverbs 11:14-KJV).* God has given many seasoned believers His wisdom. You should seek godly counsel whenever you are making major decisions or lack clarity.

5. Clear Confirmation - *In the mouth of two or three witnesses every word may be established (Matthew 18:16b-KJV).* If you continue to hear the same information from different sources, God could be speaking to you. He often confirms what He spoke to you through His Word, people, dreams, visions and/or life circumstances.

Understanding God's Voice:

Not only is hearing God's voice important, but understanding what He is saying to you is even more so. *Wisdom is the principal thing; therefore get wisdom. And in all your getting, get understanding (Proverbs 4:7-NKJV).* Understanding what you hear is key to experiencing God's desire. When God desires to warn, enlighten, guide or bless, your understanding (or lack thereof) will determine your outcome. I remember being disappointed whenever I did not properly respond to or misunderstood what God was telling me. One morning as I was putting my work bag into the trunk of my car, I suddenly had the thought: don't lay your mobile phone on the inside edge of the trunk; you will forget it is there and close the trunk. I then remember thinking, "It only takes a few seconds to throw my bag into the trunk. I won't forget that fast." Well, you can probably guess what happened. As soon as I placed my bag into the trunk, I automatically reached to close it. Unfortunately, my brand new smart phone prevented it from closing. My disregard for God's loving warning resulted in a cracked screen and a frustrated commute.

A similar example from a different occasion, I was entering my cubicle and instantly heard in my heart: *you should write your name under your chair.* I thought it was odd, but might be a good idea. I planned to get to it later. My chair was an expensive ergonomic chair. Only a select few had this type of chair, mostly executives, attorneys and those with back issues. I did not fit any category. I had been blessed that the lady who ordered my chair thought it would be a good choice for me since I would be sitting a lot. I had enjoyed the comfort of my chair for over three years. The following week I walked into my cubicle to find it had been swapped for a plain, old non-ergonomic chair. I was furious! Imagine a five-foot-six angry black woman in a business suit with high heels storming around the entire third floor hunting for a single chair. Of course, the instructions that I heard a week earlier to write my name under my chair began to replay in my head. I'm not sure if I was angrier with the person who exchanged my chair or me for not following through. I looked in every office and cubicle, asking everyone with an ergonomic chair if it was mine. After some time, I concluded I would never be able to identify or prove someone had my chair. I was disappointed with my failure to properly respond to God's voice. Now, whenever I see an ergonomic chair I think about that experience.

On another occasion, I went to Walmart to buy lip balm and a new charging cable for my mobile phone. I picked up four packs of Burt's Bees Lip Balm and walked toward the electronics section of the store. I heard in my heart: *they are going to think you are trying to steal the lip balm.* So, I made sure I held the four packs of lip balm in such a way that they stayed in clear view. I grabbed the cable and proceeded to the checkout and paid for everything. When I got home and began removing the lip balms out of their packages, one of the packages was empty. I had paid for four lip balms, but only got three. Right then I realized that I had misunderstood the voice of God. He was trying to tell me that someone had already stolen the lip balm out of the package. The lip balm cost less than four dollars. However, I was still concerned that if I misunderstood God's voice in the future the price could be much greater. I began to pray even more adamantly for a trained ear and greater sensitivity in my spiritual senses. I became desperate for an increase in understanding. I also prayed for mercy to cover my errors. I did not want to make a costly mistake in any serious matter.

I thank God that there have been many times I have heard His voice and understood. Nothing compares to the feeling of invigoration I experience when I successfully receive a transmission from Heaven. I remember driving to the store one day and hearing a person's name in my heart and suddenly feeling I would have contact with this person. As I was walking to the entrance of the store, this person came out. I was not surprised, but prepared to see them. We exchanged greetings and encouragement and went on our way. Nothing major happened, but gaining practice in exercising my spiritual senses was enough.

Another time a friend and I planned to meet for lunch. Before I started to get dressed I heard in my heart: *There is trouble, she has to cancel lunch.* Not long after God spoke I received a text from my friend that she needed to reschedule. One of her children had gotten into trouble and the police were involved. Although I had wanted to get together with my friend, I appreciated receiving the word of knowledge (the voice of God) prior to getting dressed to go and then being disappointed.

The more we listen for God's voice, the better we will become at discerning and understanding His voice. *"And your ears will hear a word behind you, saying, this is the way; walk in it, when you turn to the right hand and when you turn to the left"* *(Isaiah 30:21-AMP).* God is a present help. He is always ready and available to guide us throughout our journey. Keep your ears and heart open, and do not disregard any of your thoughts or feelings. You may not quite understand what you hear or sense, but continue to pray until you do. Moving forward without clarity can sometimes be disastrous.

Pastor Andrew Wommack's Story:

I read about an experience Pastor Andrew Wommack had that sent chills down my spine. He was planning a trip to Costa Rica, a place he had been before, and was excited to visit again. As he continued to pray about the trip, his desire began to change. The excitement he once felt had turned to dread. After seeking the Lord and praying for hours in tongues, he decided to cancel the trip. When the people of Costa Rica asked him why, all he could tell them was he no longer desired to come. It was difficult for him to let his friends down and he questioned if they understood. On the day he was to leave, the plane he booked his flight on crashed on take-off from Mexico City, killing all 169 persons onboard. God saved Pastor Wommack's life and warned him, not by saying, "Don't go to Costa Rica," but by communicating to his spirit and removing his desire to go. Remember, God communicates to us through diverse methods. He may speak to you through your desires, therefore do not dismiss or disregard them. Doing so may cost you the ultimate price, your life.

I realize that hearing about an experience like Pastor Wommack's can sometimes incite fear. Fear is always destructive and never from God. God does not want us to walk in fear of our future, but to know and trust that our life is secure in His hands. *What then shall we say to these things? If God be for us, who can be against us? (Romans 8:31-NKJV).* I have personally wrestled with the spirit of fear as I was constantly worried about what could potentially go wrong. I was so consumed with anxiety about potential tragedy in the future that I could not appreciate or enjoy the peace of the present. The power of the Living Word set me free. *"For you did not receive the spirit of bondage again to fear, but you received the Spirit of adoption by whom we cry out", "Abba, Father" (Romans 8:15-NKJV).* We have the distinct honor and privilege to call on the All-Powerful, Almighty God for help. The Creator of the universe has our back. God is near to all who call upon Him in truth. Do not anticipate God failing you. God will not make a mistake with your life. His way is perfect and His word is flawless. He will be our shield when we take refuge in Him.

Biblical Examples Of Prayer:

Throughout the scriptures are glimpses of people who remained prayerful in *The Waiting Room*. Hannah was in *The Waiting Room* through her barrenness. She was one of the two wives of Elkanah. Elkanah's wife Peninnah had sons and daughters, but Hannah was barren. In her culture, there was a shame and stigma connected to being married and childless. Year after year, Hannah was tortured by Peninnah's many pregnancies. Hannah became so vexed in her spirit that she bitterly wept and cried out to God. She made a vow to God that if He would be merciful and mindful of her by giving her a son, then she would dedicate the child to Him all the days of his life. In the process of time, God blessed Hannah and she conceived and gave birth to a son, Samuel. After weaning him, she fulfilled her vow and dedicated him to the Lord's work in the temple. Hannah's *Waiting Room* ended in victory. After Samuel she gave birth to three more sons and two daughters.

Are you burdened to the point of vexation? Is there something you desire so desperately that your life would be incomplete without it? Then cry out to the Living God and do not relent. There are things that are impossible for people, but nothing is impossible with God. He is your Creator. He is able to create the very hope that lives within you. Remain prayerful in *The Waiting Room* and never allow your hope to perish.

Another person who remained prayerful in *The Waiting Room* was Daniel. Daniel was a man of great discipline and integrity. He was envied by other high officials serving in the royal kingdom of the Chaldeans because he had an excellent spirit. Daniel distinguished himself above the other officials, and King Darius considered promoting him to reign over his entire kingdom. The jealous officials were moved to plot against Daniel to cause him to lose favor with the king and ultimately be destroyed. They could not find any fault in Daniel's leadership, so they decided to create a conflict in his worship. They consulted together and presented the king with a royal statue, stating that whoever prays to any god except the king for the next thirty days shall be thrown into the lion's den. Unaware of the plot, King Darius signed the decree into law. Daniel continued his custom of praying and giving thanks to his God even though he knew about the decree. The officials informed the King that Daniel broke the royal statue and should be cast into the lion's den. Daniel remained prayerful in *The Waiting Room* for deliverance. Even the King himself sought to find a way to spare Daniel, but could not undo his decree. Nevertheless, Daniel's prayers were answered. God sent His angel to keep the lions from harming Daniel. Those that had conspired against him, along with their families, were destroyed by the lions instead.

You may be up against an attack designed to assassinate your character and cause you to lose your good success. The demons of envy and jealousy may be stirred up against you. Be of good courage because God alone is the judge. When He promotes you, only He can demote you. No matter how scary the threats of the plot against you appear, you can overcome by God's sovereign power. Trust God and remain prayerful throughout the process and you will experience the deliverance of the Lord.

As a people, the Jews understood all about maintaining a hope while waiting for the fulfillment of a promise. For centuries, they were in *The Waiting Room* for restoration and redemption. They had a hope that somehow God would visit His people with salvation. Isaiah prophesied of the Messianic hope that existed among the covenant people: *"For unto us a Child is born, unto us a Son is given; and the government will be upon His shoulder. And His name will be called Wonderful, Counselor, Mighty God, Everlasting Father, Prince of Peace. Of the increase of His government and peace there will be no end, upon the throne of David and over His kingdom, to order it and establish it with judgment and justice, from that time forward, even forever. The zeal of the LORD of hosts will perform this"* (Isaiah 9:6-7-NKJV).

Isaiah also prophesied that a day would come when their God would come to earth, take on flesh, and become their Savior and Redeemer: *"Therefore the Lord Himself will give you a sign: Behold, the virgin shall conceive and bear a Son, and shall call His name Immanuel"* (Isaiah 7:14 KJV). The prophet Balaam said this, *"I see Him, but not now; I behold Him, but not near; A Star shall come out of Jacob; A Scepter shall rise out of Israel, And batter the brow of Moab, And destroy all the sons of tumult"* (Numbers 24:17-NKJV).

The fulfillment of these promises is found in the first chapter of the Gospel of Luke. A young Jewish virgin named Mary was engaged to be married to a young Jewish man named Joseph when her life was unexpectedly, and indefinitely, altered. *"Now in the sixth month the angel Gabriel was sent by God to a city of Galilee named Nazareth, to a virgin betrothed to a man whose name was Joseph, of the house of David. The virgin's name was Mary. And having come in, the angel said to her, "Rejoice, highly favored one, the Lord is with you; blessed are you among women!" But when she saw him, she was troubled at his saying, and considered what manner of greeting this was. Then the angel said to her, "Do not be afraid, Mary, for you have found favor with God. And behold, you will conceive in your womb and bring forth a Son, and shall call His name JESUS. He will be great, and will be called the Son of the Highest; and the Lord God will give Him the throne of His father David. And He will reign over the house of Jacob forever, and of His kingdom there will be no end." Then Mary said to the angel, "How can this be, since I do not know a man?" And the angel answered and said to her, "The Holy Spirit will come upon you, and the power of the Highest will overshadow you; therefore, also, that Holy One who is to be born will be called the Son of God. Now indeed, Elizabeth your relative has also conceived a son in her old age; and this is now the sixth month for her who was called barren. For with God nothing will be impossible." Then Mary said, "Behold the maidservant of the Lord! Let it be to me according to your word." And the angel departed from her (Luke 1:26-38-NKJV).*

Imagine what was going through Mary's mind. She was favored to be the one the prophecies spoke of and would give birth to her nation's hope for redemption. However, she now faced being disgraced as an unwed mother whose fiancé could rightfully divorce her and have her stoned. In spite of the bitter-sweetness of the moment, Mary embraced the blessing and the burden. Not fully understanding what her future held, she was still willing to do God's will. In response to Mary's submission, God began to guide her through a series of experiences leading up to the child's birth, ministry, death and resurrection.

This *Waiting Room* was intense and extensive. If anyone knew how to remain prayerful in *The Waiting Room* it was Mary the mother of Jesus. The Bible does not record any specific description of her prayer life, but, when you consider everything she dealt with in her life, fervent prayer is the only way she could have made it through. Motherhood for her was beyond eventful: angels announcing the birth of her child to shepherds in a field, a multitude of the heavenly host praising God for His birth, wise men and shepherds coming to worship Him and bringing Him gifts of gold, frankincense and myrrh. As her child grew, she was amazed by His theology and miraculous power. She watched Him gain and lead His followers, then experience persecution, false accusations and death threats. She even painfully witnessed His betrayal and death. Like many others, the hope of His resurrection lived within her heart. The final chapter of her motherhood was written after His resurrection and ascension into heaven.

Whatever your *Waiting Room* may be, prayer is key and instrumental to your success. As you go through the various stages of your journey, remain prayerful. God is the same, He changes not. Just as He was near to Hannah as she cried out for offspring, He is near to you and hears your cries. Just as He was in the lion's den as Daniel faced certain death and destruction, He is with you in your difficult circumstances. As He was with Mary while she experienced the joy and sorrows of motherhood, He is with you through anything and everything you face.

God holds your destiny in His hands. Submit your life to Him and He will establish all He has planned for your life. You do not have to fret over the challenges He allows to enter your life. He is able to guide you successfully through them all. Remain prayerful both when you feel like it and when you do not. Keep the communication established between you and God, and never allow anyone or anything to hinder it. A fully developed prayer life is a precious treasure to be cherished, guarded and enjoyed.

9

REFLECT ON GOD'S FAITHFULNESS

If we are faithless, He remains faithful; He cannot deny himself (2 Timothy 2:13 - NKJV).

Great is Thy Faithfulness is hands-down one of the most popular hymns ever written. Thomas Obadiah Chisholm wrote the hymn after struggling most of his adult life with poor health and steep poverty. Thomas found comfort in the scriptures and God's faithfulness to him during his periods of sickness and need. Lamentation 3:22-23 was one of his favorite scriptures: *"Through the LORD'S mercies we are not consumed, because His compassions fail not. They are new every morning; Great is Your faithfulness" (NKJV).*

At the end of his life Thomas recalled, although his income was never large due to his health, the faithfulness of his covenant-keeping God provided him with many demonstrations of His continuous provisions. It was out of a heart of deep gratitude that Thomas wrote the hymn "Great is Thy Faithfulness." He wrote nearly 1,200 poems throughout his life, including other published hymns.

With each new day God will give you an opportunity to experience His faithfulness. One of God's names is Jehovah-Shammah, which means the Lord is *there*. You may wonder: where is *there*? *There* is wherever you are. He is always there with you; before, during, and after you need Him. He is already at the site of your next need. He is there before you get there to need Him. You can find great comfort in the promise that God will never leave you nor forsake you. He promised to be a present help in the time of need. *"God is not human that He should lie; not a human that He should change His mind. Does He speak and then not act? Does He promised and not fulfill?" (Numbers 23:19-NIV).* The answer is no. God is, and will always be, faithful. He says, *"I am the Lord, I change not" (Malachi 3:6a).* He is completely reliable and trustworthy. His way is perfect and His word is flawless. Whatever He says, He will do. Whatever He promises, He will fulfill.

God is a God of covenant, and His relationship with man is based on a covenant. The dictionary defines a covenant as an agreement, usually formal, between two or more persons to do or not to do something specified *(Dictionary.com).* It is a pledge or a promise. God's covenant is an unchangeable, divinely imposed agreement between Him and man with conditions for the relationship. After the flood, in the days of a Noah, God made a covenant with Noah and all life on the earth. *"I establish my covenant with you: Never again will all life be destroyed by the waters of a flood; never again will there be a flood to destroy the earth." And God said, "This is the sign of the covenant I am making between me and you and every living creature with you, a covenant for all generations to come: I have set my rainbow in the clouds, and it will be the sign of the covenant between me and the earth. Whenever I bring clouds over the earth and the rainbow appears in the clouds, I will remember my covenant between me and you and all living creatures of every kind. Never again will the waters become a flood to destroy all life. Whenever the rainbow appears in the clouds, I will see it and remember the everlasting covenant between God and all living creatures of every kind on the earth." So God said to Noah, "This is the sign of the covenant I have established between me and all life on the earth" (Genesis 9: 11-17-NIV).*

Throughout the bible we read how God entered into different covenants with different people. He established covenants with Abraham, Isaac, Jacob, Moses, Noah, King David and the people of Israel. God uses covenantal relationships for a number of reasons. One reason is it is consistent with His nature. As a triune God there is a multi-faceted relationship among the Godhead. The members of the trinity are distinguished one from the others and have a hierarchy with authorities and responsibilities. There is clearly subordination within the Godhead as it relates to order. God the Father sent the Son to earth. The Son did not pursue His own will, but the will of the Father. The Holy Spirit was sent by the Son and does not speak on His own accord, but speaks only what He hears. We are created in God's image and likeness and the covenantal relationship God has with us mirrors the same process of order in the Godhead. Christ is the head of every man; the husband is the head of the wife and God is the head of Christ. Christ is the head and Savior of the church. It is God who established order in the institutions of marriage, family and the Church.

Covenantal relationship provides accountability within a hierarchy of responsibility. There are obligations and expectations placed on both parties in the relationship, with associated penalties if the obligations are not fulfilled. God has placed mankind over all of His creation and requires absolute obedience to His commandments. He placed obligations on Himself to fulfill all the promises He made in His word to care for mankind and the earth. We are all personally accountable to God according to Romans 14:10b and 12. *"Remember, we will all stand before the judgment seat of God"* and *"Yes, each of us will give a personal account to God" (NLT)*. We are also accountable to one another. As the body of Christ we are many members, but only one body. Each part is essential and has a unique function. *"He makes the whole body fit together perfectly. As each part does its own special work, it helps* the other parts grow, so that the whole body is healthy and growing and full of love" (Ephesians 4:16-NLT).

Finally, a covenantal relationship is a legally binding relationship. God is a God of law and justice. God has documented His legal covenant in written form within the Bible. God's laws, precepts, statues, ordinances and commandments provide the framework for a legally structured relationship between God and mankind. God is just and exercises justice and impartiality. He does not show favoritism or partiality. God's actions are always fair and equitable. He will fight for you when you are wronged, and correct you when you do wrong. It is man's duty to obey God's law. *"Here is the conclusion of the matter. Fear God and keep His commandments, for this is the whole duty of man"* (Ecclesiastes 12:13-NIV). The commandments of God are not burdensome or oppressive, and they can all be achieved through love. Love sums it all up. Love sums up the entire relationship you and I have with the Living God! *"Love the Lord your God with all your heart and with all your soul and with all your mind. This is the first and greatest commandment. And the second is like it: "Love your neighbor as yourself." All the Law and the Prophets hang on these two commandment"* (Matthew 22:37-40-NIV).

God's love is perfect towards you and His faithfulness is steadfast. He keeps His promises for a thousand generations, so the promises of your lifetime are secure in Him without question. The Apostle Paul wrote in Hebrew 10:23, *"Let us hold fast the confession of our hope without wavering, for He who promised is faithful"* (NKJV). When you find yourself questioning if God loves you or has your best interest in mind: take some time for reflection. Reflect on how God provided for your needs in the past. Reflect on how He helped you through your various circumstances. Reflect on all the prayers He granted and all the doors of opportunity He opened. All you need is one experience to be able to make a bold confession of God's faithfulness to you. What He did for you yesterday, He will do today and tomorrow. He does not change. Hold fast to your position of faith. Hold fast to your conclusion of God's goodness without changing your mind.

Regardless of what is happening in your life today, keep exercising faith by expecting God to act on your behalf. Part of having faith in God is expecting Him to help you and bless your life! This may be difficult, especially if you feel God has not always come through for you or acted in the way you expected. The truth is far from those thoughts. God is working in everything for your good. You might not see the final manifestation of His will in the present, but know that God will never fail you. Sometimes it is your expectations that are the problem. They can often be wrong and need to be realigned with God's will. God has done thousands of unknown things for you today. His works are so vast and His generosity so exceeding that you cannot grasp them all. He is committed to you and your life becoming all that He planned and ordained it to be. Never stop expecting from God. He will fulfill His good plans for you all the way through eternity.

Joseph's Faithfulness Story:

Consider for a moment *The Waiting Room* in the life of Joseph. As a young boy he received God-inspired dreams that revealed what would take place in his future. *Joseph had a dream, and when he told it to his brothers, they hated him all the more. He said to them, "Listen to this dream I had: We were binding sheaves of grain out in the field when suddenly my sheaf rose and stood upright, while your sheaves gathered around mine and bowed down to it." His brothers said to him, "Do you intend to reign over us? Will you actually rule us? "And they hated him all the more because of his dream and what he had said. Then he had another dream, and he told it to his brothers. "Listen," he said, "I had another dream, and this time the sun and moon and eleven stars were bowing down to me." When he told his father as well as his brothers, his father rebuked him and said, "What is this dream you had? Will your mother and I and your brothers actually come and bow down to the ground before you?"* [11] *His brothers were jealous of him, but his father kept the matter in mind (Genesis 37:5-10-NIV).* I imagine Joseph was excited about what his dreams revealed. However, he clearly did not think through how his brothers might feel about him ruling over them, and I am certain he never expected that they would do him harm. Despite being sold into slavery and thrown into prison, Joseph experienced success in whatever he did because God was with him. God was with him through every transition in his life.

Although Joseph's journey included many difficulties, he did not become discouraged or doubtful. Joseph possessed a strong faith in God. He believed God would fulfill the dreams He had revealed to him as a young boy, and He did. After interpreting the dreams of Pharaoh, the king of Egypt, Joseph experienced the fulfillment of his own dreams. *"Then Pharaoh said to Joseph, "Since God has made all this known to you, there is no one so discerning and wise as you. You shall be in charge of my palace and all my people are to submit to your orders. Only with respect to the throne will I be greater than you" (Genesis 41:39).* Joseph's father and brothers eventually did bow down to him and he became their ruler. God knew what would take place in the future and He was mindful of His people. At the end of his journey, Joseph took his last breath still trusting the faithfulness of God.

You can trust in God's faithfulness. Continue living by your faith and walking in the truth. Do not allow what you speak and what you believe to be inconsistent. The Truth says God is love. If you say God is love, but you do not believe that He loves *you*, then that is inconsistent with the truth. One of the statements is false and needs to be reconciled. How can He be love, but at the same time not love you? Either He is love and loves you, or He is not love and does not love you. You must believe God is love, and also believe He loves *you*. The Truth says God is faithful. If you say God is faithful, but you do not feel He will be faithful to *you*, then that is inconsistent with the Truth. You must believe God is faithful, and that He is faithful to you. Let your confession be consistent with the truth and walk in it. Only speak the truth and not the inconsistencies of your feelings. Say this out loud: **God is faithful, and He is faithful to me!**

My Faithfulness Story:

I often reflect on God's faithfulness to me. Usually, I do the most reflecting when I am in a difficult season. Remembering what God has done in my past helps me to endure the hardship of the present. In the early years of my journey, I remember how frustrated and fearful I would become by the first unexpected financial setback. Shortly after becoming a Christian, God blessed me with a temporary job as a receptionist for a very successful corporation. After about six months I was informed that my contract was ending and would not be renewed. Initially, I felt God betrayed my trust in Him and had let me down. I did my job exceptionally well and I expected to be offered a permanent position. I could not understand why God would not meet my simple expectation. Tears streamed down my face as I distributed the mail into personnel mailboxes. I was afraid of being unemployed and I was angry at

God for the way my job ended. At the time I was young in the faith and naïve about corporate work culture, but I eventually came to understand that life transitions were necessary and I could trust God through them all.

Months of collecting unemployment provided the perfect backdrop for me to learn humility, wisdom, and trust. Within a few months, I received a call to interview for a permanent receptionist job just down the street from the previous one. After accepting the offer, I began a fascinating journey in my faith-walk. I believe it was God's plan all along to bless me with that permanent job, but He knew I needed to take a short detour to learn some crucial faith lessons. Maybe that detour would not have been necessary if my response to being let go was in faith and not fear. Nevertheless, the wisdom I gained from the experience still benefits my life today. Every time I am confronted with disappointment my mind goes back to that day when I chose fear instead of faith. I recall the shame and embarrassment I felt after questioning God's goodness and charging Him with incompetence. Who am I to question the Living God? Who am I to become His instructor? I am His creation and every fiber of my being depends on Him.

Reflecting on how God worked in my circumstances and provided for my needs always strengthens me. I endeavor to learn each lesson well and avoid the need to repeat them. From the point God provided the permanent receptionist job to today, I can see a consistent thread of experiences in my life that reveal God's faithfulness. I worked as a receptionist for a little over a year. Then, God gave me favor with a Producer in the Video Production department who recommended me for the Production Assistant job. Learning how to film, design graphics, and edit was more of a joy than a job. I loved what I did and had a lot of fun doing it. Unlike being a receptionist, I had plenty of opportunity to work outside of the office. I attended many conferences and even had opportunities to travel.

After six years, I was informed that the company was downsizing and my position was being eliminated. This time I was ready. I knew how to respond in faith. I did not flinch or shed a tear when the Human Resources Manager pulled me into a cold, empty conference room to break the bad news. By then I understood that God was with me and He was in control of everything pertaining to my life. God once again provided for all my needs through unemployment and the generosity of people in my life. It was not long before God opened another door of opportunity, and I accepted a job managing all the media related business for an affluent municipality in a Chicago suburb.

When I reflect on God's faithfulness, I realize that, from the very beginning, God has been divinely orchestrating every transition in my life and constructing a recognizable pattern of His faithfulness. Three things stand out when I look closely at the pattern of God's faithfulness. If I had to write it as an equation it would be: Maturing Faith + Favor = God Ordained Promotion. I have included the list below to further elaborate this crucial point:

1. **God uses transitions to promote our maturity in Christ and blesses us with His favor.** *"By this my Father is glorified, that you bear much fruit and so prove to be my disciples" (John 15:8 -ESV). "Fear not, little flock, for it is the Father's good pleasure to give you the kingdom" (Luke 12:32-KJV).*

2. **God's favor usually involves connecting us with a person(s) who will be instrumental in us experiencing His planned promotion.** *"For it is You who blesses the righteous man, O Lord, You surround him with favor as with a shield" (Psalm 5:12-NASB). "For promotion and power come from nowhere on earth, but only*

from God; He promotes one and deposes another" (Psalm 75:6-7-TLB).

3. **The new promotion usually exceeds the scope (naturally and/or spiritually) of the last one.** *"His lord said unto him, Well done, good and faithful servant; thou hast been faithful over a few things, I will make thee ruler over many things; enter thou into the joy of thy lord" (Matthew 25:23-KJV).*

Take a moment to reflect on God's faithfulness in your life. Consider the various times of transition. Can you see a pattern emerging? Has God used your circumstances to cultivate and develop your faith? Has God given you favor with someone who was instrumental in opening a door of opportunity? Can you see how your growth and maturity has resulted in greater trust and greater reward? The pattern of our growth is from faith to faith (Romans 1:17) and from glory to glory ((2 Corinthians 3:18). Be encouraged and know the good work God has begun in your life will be completed. Wherever you find yourself in the process, you can rest assured that God is not finished revealing His faithfulness in your life. *The Waiting Room* is difficult, but God's grace is sufficient. As you wait for direction, provision, opportunity or help: remain faithful. *"Faithful is He who calls you and He also will bring it to pass" (1 Thessalonians 5:24-NASB).*

10

CONTINUE TO WORSHIP

Yet a time is coming and has now come when the true worshipers will worship the Father in the Spirit and in truth, for they are the kind of worshipers the Father seeks (John 4:23-NIV).

It is easy to get caught up in *just doing life* mode; being constantly busy with commitments, responsibilities, interests and pursuits. Sometimes maintaining the appropriate priorities can become difficult and we can even lose sight of the purpose for which we were created. Ultimately, we have been created to proclaim the praises of Him who called us out of darkness into His marvelous light. We are to live declaring His excellence and to be occupied with giving Him honor and praise. Through Jesus Christ a new family is born. This special family is called a chosen generation, a royal priesthood, a holy nation, and God's special possession. It is from among this family that **true worship** is experienced and true worshipers found.

Only the True and Living God is worthy of worship. Worship means to attribute worth. I love how the *Webster English Dictionary* defines it: "Worship is to honor with extravagant love and extreme submission." When you worship God you are testifying to His value, and demonstrating that He is worthy of being honored through your love and obedience. True biblical worship is first and foremost reverent. *"Therefore let us be grateful for receiving a kingdom that cannot be shaken, and thus let us offer to God acceptable worship, with reverence and awe" (Hebrews 12:28-ESV).* A true worshiper approaches worship with the understanding of who God is as He is revealed in scripture. God is holy, pure, just, powerful, everlasting, omniscient, sovereign, wise, faithful, et al. Therefore, He must be highly esteemed in your eyes in order for you to worship Him properly.

True worship is a lifestyle, not an experience. You are not worshiping simply because you are at a certain geographic location or participating in a certain ritual or tradition. You are worshiping when you invite the Living God's presence to reign in you and your lifestyle in an honorable and acceptable way. *"And so, dear brothers and sisters, I plead with you to give your bodies to God because of all He has done for you. Let them be a living and holy sacrifice—the kind He will find acceptable. This is truly the way to worship Him. Don't copy the behavior and customs of this world, but let God transform you into a new person by changing the way you think. Then you will learn to know God's will for you, which is good and pleasing and perfect"* (Romans 12:1-2-NLT). Each time you decide to live according to what pleases God, not other people or yourself, you are worshiping.

Worship is a matter of the heart. A worshipful heart is governed by the truth of the scriptures, not by external actions that can be governed by ceremony or tradition. The lifting of hands, dancing, and singing worship songs are all good activities, but do not necessarily equate worship. *"God is a Spirit: and they that worship him must worship him in spirit and in truth"* (John 4:24-KJV). True worship is accomplished only after the Holy Spirit is allowed to regenerate your spirit and begin renewing your mind by the word of truth. It is not possible to render true worship and simultaneously reject the truth of the scriptures. When you reject the truth of the scriptures you are rejecting the God of the scriptures. You cannot worship Him and reject Him simultaneously. The Father is seeking worshipers whose worship is consistently motivated by His Word and led by His Spirit both privately and publicly.

Worship & The Well:

In the fourth chapter of the Gospel of John, Jesus leaves Judea to return to Galilee, passing through Samaria en route. Scourged by the heat of the noonday sun, He sits on a well and asks a woman there if she would give Him a drink. Instead of a drink the woman gives Him a history lesson: *"You are a Jew and I am a Samaritan woman. How can you ask me for a drink?" (John 4:9-NIV).* According to first century Jewish culture Jews did not associate with Samaritans. This ideology set the stage for Jesus to teach a lesson of His own on worship. His lesson changed the woman's life, the lives of those within her city, and the lives of those generations thereafter who would seek to worship the True and Living God.

Jesus began his divine dialogue by relating to the woman's continuous task of acquiring drinking water. Her need for water and her need for true worship were about to be satisfied and clarified. She knew the facts about the water she drank and the well she drew it from. She knew the well once belonged to the patriarch, Jacob. She knew all twelve of his sons and livestock had drunk from it. What she did not know was that the one who created the well, the water, and her water pot was standing before her. She had no idea the Creator and Giver of Life was communing with her. *"Jesus answered her, "If you knew the gift of God and who it is that asks you for a drink, you would have asked him and he would have given you living water" (John 4:10-NIV).* Had she discerned that Jesus was God in the flesh and recognized that His Words contained God's power, she would have understood that His Words alone could satisfy all her needs. Jesus tells her that everyone who drinks this water will be thirsty again, but whoever drinks the living water He gives will never thirst. The living water will become in them a spring of water welling up to everlasting life. The well water could only sustain and satisfy her physical needs temporarily, but the living water could sustain and satisfy both spiritual and physical needs forever.

The woman wanted what Jesus had to offer, though for misguided reasons. Presented with this new option, she no longer wanted to settle for a drink of water from the well. *"The woman said to him, "Sir, give me this water so that I won't get thirsty and have to keep coming here to draw water" (John 4:15-NIV).* Before she could receive the life from the living water, Jesus wanted to address the life she had been living. Jesus tells her to first go and call her husband then come back. After revealing that she did not have a husband, Jesus further exposes her by saying He knows she has no husband, but has had five of them and the man she currently has is not her husband. Astonished by His insight, the woman perceives that Jesus must walk in some sort of spiritual authority. She calls Him a prophet and shifts the conversation by beginning a religious debate on the correct way to worship.

I believe this was exactly what Jesus came to discuss. Her understanding of worship was erroneous. She thought she could live in a cloud of deception and still render acceptable worship to God. She did not know her deceptive lifestyle was obstructing the power of the truth from being demonstrated in her life. Knowing and receiving the truth is vital to receiving living water. Jesus is the Truth and by His Word are we made holy. *"Sanctify them by the truth; your word is truth" (John 17:17-NIV).* We must be made holy to worship God because He is the Holy God. *"For it is written, be holy, because I am holy" (1 Peter 1:16-NIV).* The Samaritan woman was sanctified by the Truth that day and received the living water. At that moment, she no longer needed to identify with what the water from the well represented because her real need had been satisfied. What she really needed was to experience the cleansing and communion that only comes by the living water - the Truth. She left her water pot and ran to town to tell the people about her encounter with the Truth. *"Then leaving her water jar, the woman went back to the town and said to the people, come, see a man who told me everything I ever did. Could this be the Messiah?" (John 4:28-29-NIV).*

The Samaritan woman received the Truth, and the Truth set her free from everything that hindered her from experiencing true worship. She could now enter into God's Holy presence and worship Him in spirit and truth. *"God is a Spirit: and they that worship him must worship him in spirit and in truth" (John 4:24-KJV).* Is there anything obstructing your ability to offer true worship to God? Has inner discontentment driven you to seek satisfaction on your own terms? Are you attempting to satisfy your own needs through people, positions, places or things? True fulfillment is only found in communion with the True and Living God. He is the one who devised the plan and purpose for your life, so He is the only one qualified to guide and direct your path. It is His good pleasure to make known to you the good plans He has established for you, but you can only receive that knowledge in His presence. Bottom line: God desires your fellowship and delights in making your life exceedingly fruitful. *"You make known to me the path of life; in your presence there is fullness of joy; at your right hand are pleasures forevermore" (Psalms 16:11-ESV).* Worship Him daily with all your heart, mind and strength, and you will daily enjoy the endless wonders of His love.

Worship & Gratitude:

It is important to understand that true worship is characterized by a spirit of gratitude. Regardless of what has or has not happened in your life, God remains worthy. His worth and attributes never change. Circumstances, emotions, and feelings continuously change, but God never changes. He is the only constant factor in the equation of life. He is, and will always be, holy, good, faithful, just, mighty, et al. Therefore, He remains worthy of worship whether we are in the valley of despair or content in His great and precious promises.

We continue to worship God in *The Waiting Room* when we continue to trust His Word and walk in His ways despite our circumstances. Do everything with gratitude, accepting that you could never completely acknowledge or recount all of the good things God has done for you. There may be thousands of blessings you can acknowledge and recall, but I guarantee there are millions more that have escaped your understanding. *"But as it is written, eye has not seen, nor ear heard, nor have entered into the heart of man the things which God has prepared for those who love Him" (1 Corinthians 2:9-NKJV).* God loves you with an everlasting love and is continuously preparing awesome things to help and bless you. Do not let your circumstances cause you to doubt His love for you. Do not despise His grace and become ungrateful. Determine today that you will not lose heart or allow anything to weaken your will to worship. *"Worship the LORD with gladness; come before him with joyful songs. Know that the LORD is God. It is He, who made us, and we are his; we are his people, the sheep of his pasture. Enter his gates with thanksgiving and his courts with praise; give thanks to him and praise his name. For the LORD is good and his love endures forever; His faithfulness continues through all generations" (Psalms 100:2-5-NIV).*

It is always right for us to worship God. Worship Him in *The Waiting Room* the same as you would in times of peace and prosperity. Your suffering in the Lord will only last a season and will produce good fruit in your life. Do not allow despair, complaints, or anxieties to rob you of your harvest, but count it all joy and remain grateful. Let your worship spring up from your spirit and be centered in the Word of God. There is no time like the present to be the kind of worshiper the Father seeks.

11

WALK IN WISDOM

But the wisdom from above is first of all pure. It is also peace loving, gentle at all times, and willing to yield to others. It is full of mercy and good deeds. It shows no favoritism and is always sincere (James 3:17-NLT).

It should be clear by now that *The Waiting Room* will be a reoccurring experience in your life. Knowing how to walk in wisdom is a critical spiritual discipline you must develop to ensure your success. It is written, in First Samuel 18, that *"David behaved wisely in all his ways, and the Lord was with him."* God is ready to supply you with all the wisdom needed to govern your ways and bring you into good success.

One of the best strategies for ensuring that you continuously walk in wisdom is to surround yourself with wise people. The Bible teaches that with many advisors plans will succeed. You can easily identify a wise person by the way they make decisions. *"Observe the blameless. Take note of the upright. Indeed, the future of that man is peace" (Psalm 37:37-ISV)*. Wise people are known for having integrity and a good reputation. Their lives are filled with order and peace in contrast to disorder and chaos. Wise people are proficient in making sound decisions rooted in their experience, knowledge, and judgment. God has blessed me with a number of wise God-fearing people in my life. I am grateful that whenever I need advice I can reach out to either of them and receive sound counsel. *"Listen to advice and accept instruction, that you may gain wisdom in the future" (Proverbs 19:20-ESV)*. It is beneficial to have access to a diverse network of mature advisors of different backgrounds who possess a wealth of knowledge and experience.

Wisdom is highly esteemed in the scriptures and must be highly esteemed in your eyes if you want to be wise. In the eighth chapter of Proverbs wisdom is presented as a person. She declares her moral excellence and value and makes herself available to all. Even the most prominent of people rely on her. Kings and princes reign successfully by possessing her. She does not force anyone to take her, but compels everyone to desire her. You will never acquire wisdom without a desire for it. *"Does not wisdom call out? Does not understanding raise her voice? At the highest point along the way, where the paths meet, she takes her stand; beside the gate leading into the city, at the entrance, she cries aloud: "To you, O people, I call out; I raise my voice to all mankind. You who are simple, gain prudence; you who are foolish, set your hearts on it. Listen, for I have trustworthy things to say; I open my lips to speak what is right. My mouth speaks what is true, for my lips detest wickedness. All the words of my mouth are just; none of them is crooked or perverse. To the discerning all of them are right; they are upright to those who have found knowledge. Choose my instruction instead of silver, knowledge rather than choice gold, for wisdom is more precious than rubies, and nothing you desire can compare with her. "I, wisdom, dwell together with prudence; I possess knowledge and discretion. To fear the* LORD *is to hate evil; I hate pride and arrogance, evil behavior and perverse speech. Counsel and sound judgment are mine; I have insight, I have power. By me kings reign and rulers issue decrees that are just; by me princes govern, and nobles—all who rule on earth. I love those who love me, and those who seek me find me. With me are riches and honor, enduring wealth and prosperity. My fruit is better than fine gold; what I yield surpasses choice silver. I walk in the way of righteousness, along the paths of justice, bestowing a rich inheritance on those who love me and making their treasuries full"* (Proverbs 8-NIV).

Wisdom is still calling out today. Her voice is still being raised. Have you heard her calls? Have you welcomed her into your heart? Everyone who desires wisdom will receive her, and she enriches everyone who embraces her. It is true that nothing you desire can compare to wisdom. Make seeking wisdom one of the highest priorities in your life. Read, study, and meditate on the Word of God. It is from His mouth that knowledge and understanding comes. *"For the Lord gives skillful and godly wisdom; from His mouth comes knowledge and understanding"* *(Proverbs 2:6-AMP).* God says to ask Him for wisdom when you need it and He will generously supply it.

As you seek God for wisdom, be careful to approach His throne respectfully. Walking in a spirit of error will deter your pursuit, but having a teachable spirit clothed in humility will be to your advantage. Recognize your own limitations and be willing to receive correction. *"Do not be wise in your own eyes; fear the Lord and depart from evil"* *(Proverbs 3:7-NKJV).* Purpose each day to incline your ear to the voice of wisdom and apply your heart to understanding. Whenever the Lord reveals to you that the way you are going is not right, humble yourself and allow His wisdom to empower you to change.

One of my favorite scriptures is Romans 11:33: *"O, the depth of the riches both of the wisdom and knowledge of God. How unsearchable are His judgments and His ways past finding out"* *(KJV).* God's wisdom is unlimited and can never be depleted. He will provide you with all the wisdom you need to make good choices and live responsibly. Remember God is for you and He wants you to succeed. Allow His wisdom to guide your way and you will be blessed. Take the time to read these proverbs and your understanding of wisdom will increase: *Proverbs 10:8, 11:2, 12:15, 13:1, 13:14, 14:15, 20:18, 23:12, 24:6, 25:12, and 28:26.*

The Bible says to give honor to those to whom honor is due. I want to give honor to Carlton Arthurs, founder and pastor of Wheaton Christian Center church in Chicago, Illinois. I have had the privilege to attend his church and sit under his teaching for over thirteen years. His integrity is impeccable and his leadership is profound. Pastor Arthurs was born in Belize, Central America where he experienced the new birth and answered the call to ministry. With over sixty years of ministry experience, Pastor Arthurs can share a thing or two about wisdom. I decided to interview him to capture some of the great insights he has gleaned throughout his journey.

On the day of the interview I took a few minutes to share with Pastor Arthurs the vision for my book and the objective of the chapter I was interviewing him for. As I explained how well I thought he satisfied the criteria to speak on the subject of walking in wisdom, and encouraged him to share the secrets of his successfulness, I was oddly surprised by his response and assessment of his legacy. Pastor Arthurs did not consider himself to be a wise or successful person at all. I wondered how that could be possible when he is overwhelmingly regarded as such in the eyes of so many people. I know for certain if I were to ask any one of his church members whether they consider him to be wise and successful that each one would respond with a resounding yes! It caught me off guard to hear him say something completely different about himself, but by the conclusion of our interview I understood. His words changed me and I left his presence with a more sober assessment of my own sense of what it means to walk in wisdom and be successful in the Lord. I pray that his words will impact you as you read his responses.

Interview with Pastor Carlton Arthurs:

1. What does it mean to walk in wisdom?

Pastor Arthurs: It means getting, as accurately as possible, the mind and will of God and following it to the maximum.

2. How can a person recognize that they are walking in their own wisdom?

Pastor Arthurs: If it's in their own wisdom, in contrast to walking in the will of God, either life will teach you when you bump your head against that stone wall or you will simply realize that the way that you are going cannot be right because it doesn't bring the results at all that God promises.

3. Are there certain indicators that confirm a person is walking in God's wisdom?

Pastor Arthurs: The judgments of the Lord are right and the way of the transgressor is hard and the blessing of the Lord makes rich and adds no sorrow with it, in the sense that it brings God's results. It doesn't necessarily mean that it makes materially rich, but it enriches the life.

4. **What are some potential hindrances to successfully walking in God's wisdom?**

Pastor Arthurs: Following one's own impulses and appetites; a lot of times we must realize that the natural man does not receive the things of the Spirit of God, neither can he know them because they are spiritually discerned, so to get on God's wave length is the safe way.

5. **How do you personally seek God for wisdom?**

Pastor Arthurs: I do my best to get the mind of God through the Word and prayer. Then I try to expose myself to wise and successful people in the Lord.

6. **Do you have a favorite scripture on wisdom and why?**

Pastor Arthurs: I love the proverbs. They are shot through with words to the wise and admonitions to the otherwise.

7. **How have your spiritual advisors/mentors helped you be successful?**

Pastor Arthurs: I try to have a keen ear for what I believe the Spirit of God endorses from them. I don't necessarily try to copycat those whose walk with Christ I admire. The Bible advises us to walk with wise men and to mark the perfect man and behold the upright because the end of that man is peace. That is what I strive to do, not very successfully, but I do strive to do it. I don't consider myself successful by any stretch of the imagination. You are not getting advice from one who regards himself as a successful man. I'm not just saying that; that's how I deeply feel. Let's say that I'm spiritually ambitious. The things that I would love to see God do and the things that interest me, affecting humanity for Christ the way I dream of it happening in my life, I'm a million miles away from that. I have to find some place of contentment in believing that the things that elude me are things that in God's wisdom, God hasn't desired to have me experience. So I find peace in the fact that I believe that God is wise; much wiser than I.

8. What should you do if you disagree with the counsel of your advisors?

Pastor Arthurs: *I think that God has given each of us our individuality. God has persuaded us along certain lines and we kind of know that even if we think those we admire don't line up with what we already know the Lord has shown us in this world, then we reject them. We just say alright, let them find satisfaction where they find it, but I believe that God has shown me otherwise. You really try to be as discerning as you can as to what is wisdom from the wisest of men and you'll find that the wisest of men have their human faults and foibles and eccentricities and mistakes.*

9. Has there ever been a time you needed wisdom and struggled to receive it?

Pastor Arthurs: *Absolutely, that's our daily walk, I suppose. If I could wave a wand and get to where I want to go in the Lord, I would have done it long ago. It's a constant struggle; it's a striving. It's weeding out the extraneous voices that are not of God and trying to hear from Heaven. It's an intense thing. You don't stumble upon a gold mine every day and that's what we are seeking. We are seeking that hidden treasure and the Word says that we are to seek for wisdom as for a hidden treasure. So it's an intense search and an ongoing search.*

10. How can a person gain confidence in exercising wisdom?

Pastor Arthurs: Is it achievable to actually get to the place where one thinks, "Yes, I have been wise." "I have followed the wisdom of God?" I suppose you can say to some extent, but not perfectly. To begin with, you start on a journey in which God says, "My thoughts are not your thoughts, neither are my ways your ways." It's a constant assessing: what are my ways alongside God's ways? To what degree has my will been absorbed in His will?

11. What role, if any, does a person's faith play in becoming wise?

Pastor Arthurs: We have to believe that God's wisdom is attainable. We have to believe that. That's the faith aspect of it. Almighty God says if any of you lack wisdom, let him ask of God who gives to all liberally. We have to believe that God means exactly what He says and when we look back we say, "My goodness, years ago that's what I thought was wisdom, but God has infused us more and more with His wisdom." I guess that's the quest that we're on, right?

12. Would it be accurate to say that because you are a Pastor it is easier for you to walk in wisdom? Why or why not?

Pastor Arthurs: I would think that in many ways it's more difficult because if you try to please man the Bible says there's a snare in that. So, often you have to walk a lonely path. It's serious enough that we have to give account for ourselves to the Lord, but the Word of God says that if you're called to the ministry you'll give account for those over whom the Holy Spirit has made you an overseer. That is serious business.

13. In all your ministry experience, has anyone ever questioned or criticized your wisdom? If so, how did you handle it?

Pastor Arthurs: My wisdom has been profoundly questioned. I had an experience once where people said we don't want what you have, get away from us. My teachings, what I believed most seriously out of God's Word became offensive to some folk and they made me know in no uncertain terms, with very little dignity, they didn't want the likes of me or my teaching. I had a real opportunity to let hatred and resentment creep into my life. I knew that I could not have God's favor if I did that. So, I put all of their names on a piece of paper and prayed for them every day and asked God to bless them.

14. Have you ever made an impulsive decision before obtaining God's wisdom and regretted it?

Pastor Arthurs: Absolutely! I thought once that there was a girl that the Lord told me I was to marry and told her so. I missed God on it and was embarrassed to the utmost afterwards. I had to go back and tell her. It broke her heart and hurt her. Everybody who knew us knew. I was embarrassed and she was hurt. I don't know that I was following a certain strategy to get beyond it, but I just was honest before God and truthful with those who were around and acknowledged, "Look I missed it, I'm sorry. It's stupidity on my part, and it's probably the lust of the flesh that allured me to this mistake."

15. Out of the many roles you fulfill (husband, father, leader and pastor), which has been the most challenging to walk in wisdom and why? Which is the least challenging and why?

Pastor Arthurs: Being the man of God that I believe God wants me to be to my wife, I suppose that's one of the most challenging areas in my life. To love her as I know Christ loves the church. The least challenging, I suppose, accepting the fact that I am called of God. Having an unwavering confidence that I know what God wants for my life. I don't question my call. The awareness of my call is the least challenging. Knowing that when I get up in the morning, I get up to follow the calling that God has put on my life, in other words, I don't go in and out of that. I'm settled there. There is something about feeling that you have poured into your children and grandchildren adequately. Are they sold-out on Jesus? Do they think Jesus in their lives; think about pleasing Him? Are they interested in the things of God to the point where they are beginning to establish their own prayer lives and Bible study lives and watching over their own personal disciplines? Those are areas of challenge right now for me.

16. Are there any key indicators in your life that give you the assurance that you are walking in God's wisdom?

Pastor Arthurs: From time to time the Lord would make me know whether or not I'm carrying out His assignment and that would be the indicator that satisfies me. It's subjective, it's personal, and from time to time. Sometimes, He will correct my course a little and tell me here and there if I have been missing it.

17. **What are some common attacks that you have seen throughout the years that Satan uses to prevent a person from receiving or walking in God's wisdom?**

Pastor Arthurs: Lack of prayer and ignoring leadership in their lives. Refusing to come under spiritual authority when they need it and neglecting their church life. Those are things that make people never reach where God wants to take them.

18. **I feel that *The Waiting Room* concept is not only true for individual believers, but has an application for the Body of Christ collectively. As a church, we are in *The Waiting Room* for the return of Christ. How can the Church walk in wisdom to ensure readiness for the Lord's return?**

Pastor Arthurs: Be involved in the things that make for Christian growth and maturity: the Word of God and prayer, witnessing for Christ--I mean actively witnessing. When a believer matures, he has a love for lost souls and a serious desire to see someone born into the kingdom. If a believer involves himself in seeking to please God in those areas: spending time with God in prayer and in the word of God, watching over their own personal disciplines and seeking to win the lost (they will be ready).

19. **Is there a particular *Waiting Room* experience, from your journey with the Lord that you can share that would be beneficial to those who will read this book?**

Pastor Arthurs: I have strived to be involved in all of those things I mentioned, not satisfactorily, but I've known to watch over my own discipline, disciplines over my own life. To be involved in the Word of God and prayer, sustaining and living with a passion to reach others for Christ. The greatest thing that ever happened to me was that I came to realize that there is a God of infinite love and that

that love of His was personal towards me, so much so that He sent His son to die for me. Those are what I've tried to make the important things in my life.

Pastor Arthurs shared some rich, foundational insight to walking in wisdom. Being seriously active in your pursuit of Christian growth and maturity, prayer, Bible study, self-discipline, witnessing, church attendance and submission to Godly leadership are all proven to cultivate wisdom. The eighty-two years of his life experiences have fostered character and strength for others to model. I must admit, during the interview I was expecting to hear an impressive inventory of results that confirmed and celebrated his wisdom, but discovered that his wisdom is not in the things he has been able to do. His wisdom is found in the spirit in which he has done them. Pastor Arthurs' sober and gentle approach to doing the will of God is, in my opinion, the hallmark of his wisdom.

My admonishment to you is to take note of these things and do likewise. *"For now, let's hold on to what we have been shown and keep in step with these teachings. Imitate me, brothers and sisters, and look around to those already following the example we have set"* (Philippians 3:16-17-Voice).

12

FINAL ENCOURAGEMENT

Fight the good fight of the faith. Take hold of the eternal life to which you were called when you made your good confession in the presence of many witnesses (1 Timothy 6:12-NIV).

My final exhortation to you is the same exhortation the Apostle Paul gave to Timothy: *"But you, man of God, flee from all this, and pursue righteousness, godliness, faith, love, endurance and gentleness. Fight the good fight of the faith. Take hold of the eternal life to which you were called when you made your good confession in the presence of many witnesses"* (1 Timothy 6:11-12). I encourage you to flee from every enemy of *The Waiting Room* that the Holy Spirit has revealed throughout the chapters of this book. Flee from presumption, pride, discouragement, fear, anger, lust, foolishness, ungratefulness, bitterness, unforgiveness, doubt and unbelief. You do not want any of these enemies to operate in your life. If any one of them has a hold on you, repent and submit to God in obedience and that enemy will have to depart. This is how you fight the good fight of faith: flee from what is evil and pursue what is good. Pursue righteousness, godliness, faith, love, endurance, and gentleness. Through them we lay hold of eternal life.

No matter how intense the battle is, do not lose your fight! Do not lose your will to fight for what God has said is good. Do not give up in the middle of the fight you are fighting! Make sure you are in the faith and continue to fight the good fight of faith until you win. Never accept or settle for defeat. You are an undefeatable force. You are more than a conquer through Christ Jesus the Lord!

Whenever you accept or tolerate circumstances that are not God's will, you are not in the faith. Would you welcome a thief into your house and say, "Make yourself at home"? Would you tell the thief, "Take whatever you like" or "I can adjust" or "I'll get by"? That is exactly what we do when you refuse to fight the good fight of faith. At that very moment we are giving the enemy the advantage, and that should not be the case. We are predestined and chosen to win, and that is how it should be! The fight is not always easy, but it is always winnable. God has given us His living Word and His Holy Spirit to ensure our success. Live by faith and fight the good fight of faith until you secure your victory.

There is one thing that you must understand about the good fight: it is never finished. The enemy will continue to contend with you in order to bring defeat in your life. Be determined to remain disciplined and ready to engage whenever necessary. God is an ever present help. He is always with you and never leaves you or forsakes you in the battle. Follow the examples of those before you who used their faith to conquer kingdoms, administer justice, shut the mouths of lions, quench the fury of flames, and escape the edge of the sword. Maintain your confidence in the things you are hoping for; it is the assurance of those things yet to be revealed. Use your faith to defeat the enemies of presumption, pride, discouragement, fear, anger, lust, foolishness, ungratefulness, bitterness, unforgiveness, doubt, and unbelief. By your faith, you will keep your *Waiting Room* experience free of every yoke of bondage of the enemy.

As a corporate body of believers, we share a common *Waiting Room* - The *Waiting Room* for the return of Christ. *"Behold, he is coming with the clouds, and every eye will see him, even those who pierced him, and all tribes of the earth will wail on account of him"* (*Revelation 1:7-ESV*). In the twenty-fourth chapter of Matthew, the disciples asked Jesus a very important question about the sign of His coming and the end of the age. Jesus' answer was comprehensive and filled with specific details. These details are still of great significance to the corporate body of believers today. "*Jesus answered: "Watch out that no one deceives you. For many will come in my name, claiming, 'I am the Messiah,' and will deceive many. You will hear of wars and rumors of wars, but see to it that you are not alarmed. Such things must happen, but the end is still to come. Nation will rise against nation, and kingdom against kingdom. There will be famines and earthquakes in various places. All these are the beginning of birth pains. "Then you will be handed over to be persecuted and put to death, and you will be hated by all nations because of me. At that time many will turn away from the faith and will betray and hate each other, and many false prophets will appear and deceive many people. Because of the increase of wickedness, the love of most will grow cold, but the one who stands firm to the end will be saved. And this gospel of the kingdom will be preached in the whole world as a testimony to all nations, and then the end will come. "So when you see standing in the holy place 'the abomination that causes desolation, spoken of through the prophet Daniel—let the reader understand— then let those who are in Judea flee to the mountains. Let no one on the housetop go down to take anything out of the house. Let no one in the field go back to get their cloak. How dreadful it will be in those days for pregnant women and nursing mothers! Pray that your flight will not take place in winter or on the Sabbath. For then there will be great distress, unequaled from the beginning of the world until now—and never to be equaled again. "If those days had not been cut short, no one would survive, but for the sake of the elect those days will be shortened. At that time if anyone says to you, 'Look, here is the Messiah!' or, 'There he is!' do not believe it. For false messiahs and false prophets will appear and perform great signs and wonders to deceive, if possible, even the elect. See, I have told you ahead of* time. *"So if anyone tells you, 'There he is, out in the wilderness,' do not go out; or, 'Here he is, in the inner rooms,' do not believe it. For as lightning that comes from the east is visible even in the west, so will be the coming of the Son of Man. Wherever there is a carcass, there the vultures will gather. "Immediately after the distress of those days, the sun will be darkened, and the moon will not give its light; the stars will fall from the sky, and the heavenly bodies will be shaken. "Then will appear the sign of the Son of Man in heaven. And then all the peoples of the earth will mourn when they see the Son of Man coming on the clouds of heaven, with power and great glory. And he will send his angels with a loud trumpet call, and they will gather his elect from the four winds, from one end of the heavens to the other"* (Matthew 24:4-27-NIV).

It is evident within the current culture that many of the things Jesus foretold have happened or are happening right now! Wars, rumors of wars, and natural disasters continue to take place in various locations throughout the earth. Persecution has undoubtedly intensified and fosters great fear among many people, especially people of faith. Sadly, countless lives have and will be taken for the sake of the faith, causing many to depart from believing. Unfortunately, hate and betrayal are increasing, while love and faithfulness are on the decline. The cause of all these troubles can be traced to the progression of wickedness that festers in the heart of man. The warning for you and me is *to not allow these grievous experiences to rob us of love.* And that, my friend, will be tough. Only those who are determined and intentional about walking in love will succeed.

No sane person likes being mistreated or enjoys watching someone else mistreated. There is something innate within each of us that desires and demands justice. Even when we do something wrong we are keenly aware of what is right. God created us that way. The question we must all ponder is how can we keep love

116

from growing cold when we or people we know are victims of hate? How can we abide in love while experiencing severe suffering, deliberate mistreatment, or unprovoked attacks? *"With man this is impossible, but with God all things are possible" (Matthew 19:26-NIV).* You will not succeed at abiding in love with your own understanding or in your own strength. It requires the mind and strength of the Lord. We must pray and ask the Lord to give us His divine understanding and His supernatural strength to walk in love; that is exactly what it will take to endure in these last days.

We are living in dark and difficult days and it is highly improbable that anyone is unaware of the brutal hatred that permeates our society. The naked reality is that hate is extremely destructive and causes a multitude of hurt and pain, but the solution to hate is love. *"Above all continue to love each other deeply, because love covers a multitude of sins" (1 Peter 4:8-ISV).* Imagine the impact that you will make when you are confronted with hate, but endeavor to show love. Your life, as well as the lives of others, will be greatly transformed. The more people endeavoring to walk in love, the greater the triumph over evil will become. Let us not walk around judging sin, but covering sin with love. Love is better than judgment. God is love and just as He has reconciled you to Himself through Christ, He has given you the responsibility to reconcile others. *"And all this is a gift from God, who brought us back to himself through Christ. And God has given us this task of reconciling people to Him" (2 Corinthians 5:18-NLT).*

As members of the body of Christ, without exception, we must walk in love. Love is the link that unites the family of faith. Love identifies believers as Jesus' disciples. *"By this all men will know that you are my disciples, if you have love for one another" (John 13:35-NASB).* The body of Christ is made up of many parts, and each part has its own special function and purpose. Each part needs the other parts' contribution to be effective. No part can boast within itself and every part should be concerned for the others. God has given us different gifts according to His grace. If your gift is the gift of service, serve with love. It does not matter what the gift is: teaching, prophesying, giving, encouraging, leadership, etc. Be sure to do it with sincere love.

The scriptures make clear what love is and what love does. *"Love is patient, love is kind. It does not envy, it does not boast, it is not proud. It does not dishonor others, it is not self-seeking, it is not easily angered, it keeps no record of wrongs. Love does not delight in evil, but rejoices with the truth. It always protects, always trusts, always hopes, always perseveres. Love never fails"* (1 Corinthians 13:4-8-NIV). God's love is perfect, pure and powerful. It is God's love that enables a person to demonstrate these honorable traits. The more you possess God's love, the more you will exhibit the characteristics outlined in 1 Corinthians 13. I believe that when Jesus Christ returns for His bride, the thing that will distinguish her from the world will be God's love. Jesus will recognize His bride, the Church, by the love of the Father adorning her. When the church is complete in God's love, she will be ready for the bridegroom. When the people of God are fully walking in God's love, the door of the *Waiting Room* will open and the bride will be invited to enter into eternity with the bridegroom. I am persuaded that it is love that will facilitate the readiness of the church for the Lord's return. Until that glorious day comes, let each of us be diligent in doing our part in love so that the church will grow and be healthy. *"Instead, we will speak the truth in love, growing in every way more and more like Christ, who is the head of his body, the church. He makes the whole body fit together perfectly. As each part does its own special work, it helps the other parts grow, so that the whole body is healthy and growing and full of love"* (Ephesians 4:15-16-NLT).

Continue to ponder the things you have read and apply the wisdom you have gained to every *Waiting Room* experience. Remember, *length of time* should never be your focus, but *making decisions* that are motivated by faith in God. No matter how long the process takes or how difficult the process becomes, remain love-conscious. Be devoted to walking in love to the very end, knowing that God will cause all things to work together for your good. I'll leave you with one last word of encouragement from the scriptures. Hold fast and meditate on these words of comfort whenever you feel overwhelmed in *The Waiting Room* or feel that your love is growing cold: "*Our suffering is light and temporary and is producing for us an eternal glory that is greater than anything we can imagine*" *(2 Corinthians 4:17-GWT)*. May God abundantly bless your *Waiting Room* experience and grant you the victory of every promise of His Word!

www.ingramcontent.com/pod-product-compliance
Lightning Source LLC
Chambersburg PA
CBHW061957040426
42447CB00010B/1786